The Fruit That Is Ripe Is Always Sweeter

The Gospel of Peace

Treva Scott Thompson

WESTBOW
PRESS®
A DIVISION OF THOMAS NELSON
& ZONDERVAN

WestBow Press books may be ordered through booksellers or by contacting:

WestBow Press
A Division of Thomas Nelson & Zondervan
1663 Liberty Drive
Bloomington, IN 47403
www.westbowpress.com
1 (866) 928-1240

ISBN: 978-1-9736-5451-3 (sc)
ISBN: 978-1-9736-5452-0 (hc)
ISBN: 978-1-9736-5450-6 (e)

Library of Congress Control Number: 2019902056

Print information available on the last page.

WestBow Press rev. date: 4/17/2019

Dedicated to my children:

My daughter: Joni Lynn Soale,
Joni has been so supportive, patient and
Helpful during the writing of this book.
My son: Brent Eugene Soale
And family.

Contents

Introduction... ix

Journey of a Soul Set Free.......................................1

Inspirational Poems and Essays 27

We can Conquer Fear...99

Embracing Our Spirit Is The Essence of Life 149

Introduction

I am the fifth child in a family of eleven children. We were reared in a Christian home, where our parents showed their love for us. We attended church three or four times a week.

I have sought God since I was a small child. I remember when I was around five years old, my older brother had appendicitis. I got a stack of handkerchiefs (we didn't have Kleenex then), got down by my little chair, and cried and prayed for him to be healed. The whole congregation prayed for him to be healed. God healed him.

I grew up with an unhealthy fear of God. To my knowledge, my brothers and sisters didn't seem to fear what the preacher said as much I did. We heard more condemnation preached than we heard of God's love. Since church and God were such big parts of my life, fear was always there.

After marrying and having two children, we went to church and they heard the same preaching. During these years I sought God for answers to my fears.

I found it is the love of God that brings us to him. The preaching used fear to bring us to God. Fear always fails when it is brought to light. Fear did not bring life to my soul.

God's Word burned inside me and brought life-giving words to live by and taught me not be afraid. I was then able to show my children that God is love and will always be their friend, and not to fear God.

As I was searching and finding peace in my heart and soul, the following poems began to come forth. Every word that came to me I wrote down as fast as I could. I spent years and many reams of paper writing what God gave me to heal my troubled mind. Rather than keep all the writings in a box on a shelf, I felt God would want me to share with others. I hear so many people have the same fears I had. I want the reader of my book to come away knowing that God is love, not fear.

I guess I could say that I wrote myself out of darkness into God's light. I have many writings of peace and comfort. My prayer is that you never lose hope.

Journey of a Soul Set Free

The Flight of a Soul

I am a child, emotionally
Bound with chains, struggling,
Afraid to move, without any confidence!
I only feel a very slight glimmer
Of hope in my soul.
No one to turn to!
No one to listen!
No one understands!
All are convinced what they
Believe is right, not to be questioned.
Still, in my soul, there must be
An answer.
There must be freedom.

Surely God loves me.
Why doesn't He love me?
I love God!
No, I am afraid of God!
I will never be able to please Him.
I am nothing, just striving to be me.
I am only a child.
How would I know anything?
Why would I even question?

Now I will have to ask
Forgiveness.
For God doesn't love me.
If God doesn't love me,
Then who does?
I don't have anything to say.
Nothing anyone would want to hear.
I am nothing.

I have never had a chance to disagree.
Just to ask questions. "Please, just hear me."
No one ever thinks of listening.
I am a child with
An emptiness in my soul.
Wait, I do have feelings!
I do wonder.
I do feel God.
I do know there must be more.
I feel differently.
I must be wrong
Since I feel this way.
I would be all right if I felt like
Others felt.
I must be wrong.
Something is wrong with me.
Maybe I have sinned the
Unpardonable sin.
Maybe God will never love me.
I want to go to heaven.
I do believe in God.
God, I do believe.
Please, help my unbelief?

You said if we ask for bread (Matt. 7:9 KJV)
You would not give us a stone.
You said ask, seek, and you will find.
God, I am asking; I am seeking.
Please, God, hear me.
Heal me, heal my thinking.

Oh, God, help me for I have sinned.
I don't know what I have done,
But surely I wouldn't feel this way
If I had not sinned, would I?
The nights of torment, pain, and fright
After hearing preachers tell us
We are, "Weighed in the balance
And found wanting" (Dan. 5:27 KJV).
God, what can I do?
Don't you love me; what can I do?
How can I get you to love me?
I am at church every time the
Doors are open.
I pray before I eat.
I pray before I go to sleep.

I am so alone.
No one seems to understand.
I go to school and feel alone.
I don't feel equal to the other
Children.
I feel less of a person.
They seem to be happy.
I am laden, burdened, bound, and
Withdrawn.

I am told that God is love.
Well, I haven't seen or felt any love.
I lie awake at night,
Afraid of what might happen.
Is something wrong with me?
I am so different!
My hair is long.
I can't cut my hair.
A preacher once told me my
Hair is my glory!
He said I need to do this and to
Do that so God will love me.
Surely I can be good!
Surely God will love me!
I do not believe anyone else feels as I feel.
There is no one to listen when I
Say how I feel.
Even though I go to the altar every
Sunday night
To confess for what I have
Said or done,
No one ever tells me that God loves
Me just as I am.
No one to put their arms around me.
There was no one offering comfort
To my weary soul.
There is no one who understands.
I am the only person who feels this way.
I do not have any personality, like
A doll without a face.
A heavy cloud hangs over my head.
Religion—the only reason for living?

Or could it possibly be that
Believing God was more important?
It seemed going to church was the
Only right thing to do.
I was not receiving any spiritual food.
I was in church three or four times
A week; I would listen to sermons
Of fear and condemnation.
I feared I was not serving God if I
Didn't go to church each time the
Doors were open.
The neighbor's kids seemed happy
Even though they did not attend church.
Of course, we were told that they
Could not go to heaven if they did
Not attend church.
Well, I didn't want to be a sinner.
I didn't want to end up in a place of torment
To burn forever and ever!
Strange, very strange, a miracle happened.
When I was eight or nine years old,
I began to read a set of books I found in the library.
I have probably read all of them.
I can understand when I look back
Why I was so fascinated by the stories.
They were stories about children
With trials and conflicts that
Turned their lives into hope, faith,
And courage.
I received encouragement that
Burned within me.
I could not quit reading the

Exciting stories.
I began to have a vision that this
Could happen to me.
That desire to find the truth grew
Even stronger.

When I was old enough to start dating,
I didn't have anything to say.
All I knew was church.
I was bound by fear.
I was afraid no one would listen to
What I had to say.
I was not an individual.
I was just an extension of the family.
I existed; that was all.
I married a year after graduation
From high school. The first week
We arrived home from our honeymoon,
And trouble broke loose.
I had forgotten to get the key for a
Rented house where we were to
Start our new life together.
My husband accused me of
Intentionally forgetting the key.
I wasn't aware I was supposed to
Have the key.
How could I intentionally forget it?
I did not know how to cope with
His anger.
Growing up with my brothers and sisters,
We were never allowed to have
A disagreement.

How was I to know how to deal
With such a conflict or solve a problem?
I cried for hours!
How could someone love me and show such anger?
I had never witnessed my father or
Mother having a disagreement.
As far as we children knew,
Our parents never disagreed.
I thought if you loved someone,
You would get along with them
Without showing so much anger.
I started my marriage by being
Scarred for a long time
Over that one experience.
I never knew how to stand up for
What I believed was right.
Our parents provided for our needs.
They loved us very much.
I lacked the knowledge to face life's challenges.

I began to study the Bible for myself.
I prayed, "God, dear God,
Show me what you are really like."
The scriptures began to take on a
Different meaning as I read the
Word for myself.
I found light, not darkness.
There was life, not death.
It was uplifting, not browbeating.
There was a reason for living,
Not a reason for dying!
I found tools to live by.

Finally, I was not alone!
The kingdom of God was within me.
Jesus came to show me what
It was like
To be a child of God—
Peace, rest, comfort, love, and joy.
I am a spirit, the same as God is a spirit.
With God's Word,
I can free myself of fear, guilt,
And condemnation.
I began to interpret the scriptures
As they were written,
Not the way I had been taught.
I was afraid to believe what I was
Reading.
Maybe I was being rebellious.
Maybe I had the wrong spirit.
Maybe, just maybe I was wrong.
I didn't know anyone who
Believed like I believed.
Little by little, I became rooted in
My beliefs; His words were life to me.
I found that we are all God's children.
Some are more rebellious than others,
But we are still His children. Jesus
Did not die in vain.

We may squander our inheritance.
He still receives us back with open
Arms.
My mind was my worst enemy.
My thoughts overshadowed the

Truth by the beliefs of the rites, rituals,
And traditions of humankind.
I was finding life with God's love
Is fulfilling.
God loves me just the way I am!
He just loves me!
He did not quit loving me!
His love is forever!
Nothing I can do can stop His
Love for me.
God is love.
This has been a long journey,
Searching until I found life.
I have found peace, rest, and
Comfort.

One thing I can declare
Without a doubt,
God loves me!
The day I realized that truth,
I cried like a baby.
I believe my soul was cleansed;
My eyes were opened.
God had been there all the time.
I just didn't know the truth.
I wrote a poem that day that sums
Up the flight of my soul:

The Master's Touch

The sweetest music
On this earth
Is the tug of the heartstrings
By the lowly birth.

The heart that is yearning
For a little rest,
When strummed by the
Master's hand is at its best.

The soul is cleansed
And lifted above
By the vibrations
Of peace, joy, and love.

The Master's touch
Is all that is required
For the soul to sing
In the angelic choir.

I felt an unconditional love for the first time.
I have a love that would keep me strong.
I am worthy because I am a child
Of my Creator.
I continue to enjoy the love and
Peace that God has to offer.
I like to share my experience
With others who are searching for God's love.

God's Perfect Plan

God's perfect plan for my life is
Too magnificent for me to realize.
I must walk one step at a time;
Looking ahead would be too
Great to grasp all God's
Mercy He has ready to unload.
Would be too wondrous
For this earthly temple to enfold.

Children of God

My mother gave birth to
Eleven children.
We do not act alike.
We do not look alike.
We do not believe alike.
But nothing can take
Away from the fact
We are all her children.

God is life!
Since we have life,
God is our Father.
We are all His children.
We do not think alike.
We do not believe alike.
God does not disown anyone.
It is because of our thinking
If we are separated
From our God.

He loves us all, and
He gave us all life.
He gave us all a measure of faith.
We can plant and reap abundantly.
We do not have to go through
Forms and rituals.

No striving to get good enough to
Be accepted. Our mind separates
Us from complete fellowship with
Our heavenly Father.
God is waiting to be recognized
In the chambers of our souls.

Breath of Life

Why hasn't someone told me
The story my soul has longed to hear?
The words of peace and goodness,
Of joy that rings so clear.

Why hasn't someone told me
I have life and life so new?
Why hasn't someone told me
The longing in my heart will not do?

The bondage of my mind
Has hindered the flow of love
And faith so near.
Why hasn't someone told me
I don't have to be doomed by fear?
Freedom from within, there is
Where peace begins.

With each breath of life, I'm free.
Free from the bondage where I
Have been. Freedom from within.
My soul has wings.

God Is There

In whatever situation
I find myself,
God is there!
Lonely and sad,
With burdens to bear,
God is there!

Sickness and death
Lurking near my door,
I can look up and
Know for sure
God is there!

Rejoice! Rejoice!
What glorious peace
Sweeps over my soul
Knowing God
Is my Father, and His love
I can behold.

It is a wondrous truth!
With others
I can share
When I truly realize
God is there!

The Joy of Freedom

There are some things I cannot
Change: my father, mother,
Brothers, sisters, and my relatives.
Many situations in life can be changed.
I can give control to others
When I am the one
Who needs to be
Making those decisions.

I can say I don't have any control
As to what happens to me.
I do have control.
It takes an effort to take control of
Whatever happens to me.
This may be the hardest task
I will ever have to do.
That is, if I do a good job.

I can change the place where I live.
I can change the place where I work
And change the things that I do.
I can change the car that I drive,
Clothes that I wear,
And the food that I allow myself
To eat.
I may or may not marry.
I plan how many children to have
And how to rear those children.
By naming all these things,

It appears I have control of almost
Everything that is in my life.
The truth is, I do have control.
I may not realize that truth
Unless someone calls it to my attention.

I can get stuck in the same old rut,
Telling myself there is not
Anything I can do about
My lot in life.
When the fact may be
I do not possess the energy or
Knowledge
To do anything differently.

Changes are hard to make.
I can stay miserable
Because I believe someone may
Not agree with my decisions, or
Changes.
In the end, it matters not
What someone else will think.
It is in my choosing.

True, it may be a struggle to change,
But the rewards are great.
I have control of only
One person—myself.
Fear and fear alone is the one
Thing that keeps me from taking that control.
Fear of the unknown, fear of
Failure, fear as to who may or may

Not care;
Fear is linked to whatever is
Keeping me from making changes in my life.

The thought of fear
Causes the emotions of fear and doubt.
Faith can replace fear and doubt.
Faith is the greater force.
I can gain momentum
When I allow faith to guide me.
Fear hinders and binds
By causing me to draw back
And keeping me from opening
New doors.
Faith leads and guides by directing
My path with confidence.
There is freedom
When I open my life to faith
In whatever I allow myself to do.
There is security in faith and confidence.
I can choose to go through life
Floating downstream,
Never knowing the strength
I would gain
By swimming and going
Against the current.
By going upstream,
I can experience the joy of freedom.
I am becoming a whole person.
I am willing to stand up for whatever
I believe to be right, and be
Honest with myself.

Living one way
When I know to
To live another way
Is not allowing myself
To experience the joy of freedom.
I was not born to live in fear.
I was born to have love,
Power, and a sound mind.

A Privilege

What a privilege to know
Someone who never points a finger
Nor let His anger show.
He leads the way
When the path is dim.
We have only to lean and trust in Him.
Not one of His own has He ever forsaken.
Have courage now; your burden He has taken.
Trod up the hill to Calvary's tree,
Each step He took was for you and me.
He came to do His Father's will,
Preaching and praying and healing the ill.
Loving and caressing the homesick and sad,
The Good Shepherd loved all.
He was a friend to the good and bad.
He said He would have mercy
And not sacrifice His love.
So one can be found
And brought to the fold,
Where God's peace and joy abound.

A Simple Plan

Salvation is by faith.
Just look up and receive.
God looks on the heart.
You have only to believe.
Humankind has complicated God's
Simple plan.
Salvation is free.
He holds it in His hand.
Does love rule and reign as you see His plan?
Does peace sweep over you
When the storms are raging high?
Is there calm when others can only sigh?
As He listens to you
He has for you prepared the best?

Why should Jesus listen to me?
I don't deserve His peace.
Why should I believe?
I have nothing to lose, everything to gain.
I'm going to believe as my doubts begin to wane.

God cares for me, and I am to believe
That He died to redeem me back to fellowship
With Holy Creator.
You may not see the change, but
Believe me, I'm free. Free from worry,
Free from despair and strife.

Free from the fear
That has hampered my life.
Free from the guilt of sin and shame
Jesus is the One. Jesus is His name.

Inspirational Poems and Essays

I have learned during my search for peace that the greatest love story known to mankind is the wooing and waiting of God's love in each life.

No Greater Love

No greater love hath man than this,
That he lay down his life for his
Friends.

Go tell that man who spat in my face,
In my kingdom I've prepared for
Him a place.
If he had known of my matchless grace,
He never would have spat in my face.

Yes, go find who made the crown of thorns.
When placed on my head,
Oh, how the blood did flow.
Tell him that blood can save his soul.
How it can cleanse and make him whole.

Search out that one who drove the
Spear into my side.
There's a closer way to my heart
Than through the outside.
Give him a scepter instead of a spear
If he will accept my love that is near.

Bring those men who for my
Garments cast their lots.
Tell them a mansion is waiting
Free from cost.
Spotless white robes will be furnished
If they can believe
I am King of all Kings
No greater love, hath man than this,
That he lay down his life for his friends.

Love Is the Secret

Love is the secret!
Love is the answer to all questions.
Love does not fail us.
Love conquers all.
Love and faith dwelling within are
Precious gifts.
Love is the stronghold.
I would that you be in health and prosper.
You are free to prosper.
You are free to be in health.
You are free to love yourself.
You are free to be good to
Yourself.
Being good to yourself
Is not being selfish.
You are free to love.
You are free to be you.
Free to think.
Free to make decisions. Yes!
Love is the secret.
When you find love, you will find yourself.

Room in the Inn

Our American flag is being displayed
In windows, on cars, and on lapels.
A few months ago, we only saw
Flags displayed on holidays.
Today they are everywhere.
Why?
When push comes to shove, we are
A chip off the "old block."
Our forefathers came to America
To worship as their spirits led.
They knew the importance of
Always following their spirits;
Wherein lies the core of life.

We were a spirit before we were born.
That measure of faith is in each and
Every one of us.
We draw on that faith that will
Never let us down.
Never lets us down!
What about all the death and violence?
Fathers and mothers, sons and
Daughters didn't come home.
We are left with grief, sorrow,
Pain, disappointment, and hardships.
That ever-loving spirit cries with us,
Aches with us, suffers with us,
And never leaves our side.
We were not promised that we

Would not have tremendous
Burdens to bear,
But we do have a Comforter to
Help us endure that pain.

I think we all felt a sense of
Righteous indignation rising up
Within our spirits when the
Terrorists threatened our freedom!
How dare they think our faith
Would be shattered by anything
They could possibly do!
The bravery of our grandfathers,
Fathers, mothers, sons, and daughters
Have endured; they are still
Willingly protecting that freedom.
I would like to think if Joseph
And Mary were searching for a place
To lay Jesus this Christmas Eve
There might be "room in the inn"
(Luke 2:7 KJV).
I would hope many doors
Would be open to welcome the King.

Diamond

You found a little pebble
That lay beside the road.
It was not a thing of beauty;
It was just another stone.
Bruised and battered, chipped and worn,
It was just a little pebble that lay beside the road.
You picked it up and looked at it closely.
Somehow it was different.
It had a special glow.
With just a little polish and a little care,
Maybe that worn pebble
Wouldn't look so bare!
You told me you loved me.
Said you even cared.
You didn't want to lose me.
Gently, you held me there.
I was that little pebble
That had fallen alongside the road.
You made me feel worthy
To stand by your side; for now,
I am that diamond, glowing with pride.

Yesterday's Tears

Yesterday's tears hold joy for
You tomorrow.
Yesterday's tears will wash
Away all your sorrow.
Only My love, soon you'll see.
Have no fear.
Yesterday's tears bring joy to
You tomorrow.
Yesterday's tears wept in sorrow.
Yesterday's tears bring peace to you tomorrow.
Only peace you will see; peace is very near.
Yesterday's tears bring peace to you tomorrow.
Yesterday's tears come from a
Heart so empty.
Yesterday's tears will soon be
Forgotten.
The light breaks through; the night is past.
Yesterday's tears
Bring joy and peace at last.

Commitment

We can think, plan, dream, and talk.
Until we put works with our faith,
Nothing can happen.
In the valley of decision is
Dissatisfaction.
Dissatisfaction can be the door to
Something better for us.
Ask, and you shall receive.
Seek, and you will find.
Knock, and the door will swing open.
How bad do I want something?
What will I do to attain it?
Why do I want it?
Am I willing to search until I receive?
I will succeed.
I have only to try!

We are born with passion.
Commitment, dedication,
Consecration, and determination
Will awaken our passions.
When we commit to winning,
We can reap the joy.
We need each other.
What one of us can't supply, the
Other one can.
We will try all kinds of excuses to
Escape from doing what we want to do.
We are really our worst enemies.

When we commit our passions to a
Cause, those same energies begin
Working for us.

We are a workable force. Each
One of us is both spirit and human.
We can tap into that higher power
That dwell's within,
And we can find our
Hearts' desires.
That powerful resource can put
Legs to our wishes
And can create peace in
Hearts and minds.

Only Believe

My peace shall flow like a river
On land and sea.
My peace shall flow like a river.
Look up and believe!
My grace is enough.
It will see you through.
My grace is enough,
Always holding you true.
Mercy holds my people.
Look up and believe!
My mercy holds my people
On land and sea.
My children have perfect peace.
They have perfect peace
On land and sea.
My children have perfect peace.
They have only to believe!

Climbing

Day of darkness,
Fear gripping our souls.
Our thoughts are tied in knots,
While wanting to free our minds.
Somehow we know we will find our way.
We travel onward and upward,
Searching for truth while
Gripping to the side of the path
As we reach for footholds.
We are going where some brave
Soul has trod before.
The brave will dare go beyond
As we search for His light.
Little by little, we inch our way,
Gaining ground.
We stop only to rest but not being content.
As we reach out, the valleys may
Be even deeper, and the mountains
May reach a little higher
As we find new life springing forth.

Be Proud, America!
March On

America! America!
The land of the free.
Freedom from slavery and
Freedom to vote.
Freedom to think and speak as we belong.
It is a blessing to lie down at
Night and not hear bombs blasting
Or sirens screaming.

We can move about freely, doing
What we desire to do.
We can fulfill our dreams,
Accomplish our hopes and desires, and
Reach out to help and be
Willing to be helped.

America! America! The home of
The brave.
Develop courage to attain
The goals we have set,
Then we can leave a heritage of love.
Develop courage to be what
Our consciences bid us to be.
We know that brotherhood stems
From our own self-respect.
We are a nation of freedom-
Loving leaders and troops.

May our hearts' prayers and
Actions reflect our gratitude to all
Who protect our liberties.

Courage is simple faith that is
Coupled with works to sustain us.
"Oh, say can you see by the
Dawn's early light?"
What do we see for America?
Freedom is meant for one and all.
Freedom was not meant to
Harm our fellow humans
With liberty comes responsibility.
Look within for the courage to be free.
When discrimination is present
Among us, we belittle the cause.
Commitment will give us many
Happy returns, America.
Stand tall, America, march on!
Great people have left
Footprints upon the sands of time.
Their courage and faith make way
For our tomorrows.
The horizon is even more
Challenging as it lights our path.
Be proud, America! March on!

Christ with Me

"Christ go with me and stay by my side,"
I have sometimes begged and cried.
I believe I have missed the mark.
His light ever shines, but I am still
In the dark.
Christ is with us each hour of the day.
Not recognizing Him is our own dismay.
For He is a friend who sticks closer
Than a brother.
He cannot fail for there is none other.

We Settle

Sometimes we may settle for
Feeling like we are less of a person
Than we want to be.
We do not feel whole.
We feel different.
We feel like something is beyond our control.
We become obsessed with this thing.
We do not believe there is hope.
We can be in control of our lives.
We need to be willing to face our fears.
There is hope!
Fear is at the root of our thinking.
Fear is very real, the same as
Confidence is very real.
Fear destroys our lives, but
Confidence enriches our lives.
The moment we decide that we
Will not entertain those negative
Thoughts, they will disappear.

God Is with Us

God is in each life, showing the
Way to be loving and wise.
Gentleness and long-suffering are
One and the same,
Not pushing or shoving to make
For us a name.

We are waiting and watching,
And wanting to please
The Creator of the universe, who
Heals our dis-ease.
Struggling and striving, we are
Never satisfied it seems.
Always wanting something more
As we continue to seek an open door.
Being content with what we possess
Shall rid our lives of envy,
Bitterness, and stress.
Each of our talents
Are unique indeed,
Lifting the fallen, strengthening
The weak.

We begin to lead
By loving, guiding, and
Delivering many out of the
Bondage of fear and deceit,
Ever waiting and watching to
Relieve burdens of fear and greed.

Wholeheartedly lifting the
Burdens of others
As we loosen the bands of
Wickedness, condemnation, and sin.
Always searching for the truth
And shedding light along the way,
Knowing peace on earth
And goodwill will continue
To ring across the land.

Lonely and Sad

You say you are wretched, lonely, and sad.
I have good news to make you glad.
Jesus never turned anyone away
Who knocked at His door
Without any money to pay.

God's gifts are free; Jesus paid the price.
All we do is look up with faith and try
Try to grasp the depth of His love
To redeem us back to fellowship
With our Maker up above.
Jesus was that lifeline, thrown out
Into the deep.
Before, there wasn't any hope.
We could only weep.
Jesus came to dry our tears,
To take us in His arms and calm our fears.
His words are life; they never return void.
Take hope today and just a little Faith employ.

Peace and Contentment

Terror, torment, confusion, and doubt—
All are common in this world throughout.
Peace and contentment are hard to find
Among all the strife,
Envy and greed that blinds.
To think material wealth can
Supply my needs is a sad story and ends only in grief.
That empty place within my soul
Can only be replaced by a life that is sold,
Sold out to Christ 100 Percent!
Sold out, I say signed over to Him!
Maybe He can make something useful of me,
So that not me, but He, others will see.

I Love You!

Oh, Jesus, I love Thee.
Perfect peace Thou dost give.
Oh, Jesus, I praise Thee.
Upon the housetop let it be said,
"Hold fast to what you have.
Go on in, and open the door
To a greater life
Than you have ever known before."

The Mind

The mind can be one's worst enemy.
It can tear down and destroy by degree.
It isn't something imaginary.
It is real; please believe
God has promised us a sound mind.
Let's hold on until it comes
For everything He has promised
His blood has won.
Think about His goodness.
Think about the love He offers on
Wings of prayer.
If we are afraid, it came not from God.
Cast it aside.
Let trust upon it trod.
You can't find anyone He has
Failed?
He comes to take away our fears
As He calms our torment.

When God Speaks

I cannot express His love I feel.
He is so good and divinely real.
His presence surrounds us;
With His goodness we are engulfed.
He speaks to our souls
With whispers so soft.
He gently leads us step by step,
Stretching forth His hand,
Lifting us out of each depth.

Trials and Tests

When we have trials,
Temptations, and tests?
God can show forth His
Righteousness.
We are His children, made in His
Very likeness.
We are meek and lowly,
Long-suffering with gladness.
Be a friend to the poor, and care
For the weak.
Encourage the weary;
Take care of the meek.
There is something each one can do.
Seek God first, His will to show you.

Showers of Blessing

Showers of blessings are awaiting all
Who kneel at the cross and answer the call.
Faith in our hearts has no boundary lines.
Without faith in God, we are spiritually blind.

One Word

Is there just one word I can say
That will help someone today
Who feels life just isn't worth living?
No one cares or looks their way.
There is hope, glorious hope
For God's arm is not shortened.
His love to behold
Is the next door to open.
Don't give up when all hope is gone.
Remember, there is a rainbow
After the storm.

Thank You

Thank You, Lord, for this new day.
Whatever it holds, I won't be dismayed.
Thank You for keeping me safe all
Through the long night.
Among Your many children,
You held me in Your sight.

The Master's Cry

Hold the banner high.
Wave the flag today.
Hold the banner high.
Let come what may.
I will fear no evil, and
To only do good is my desire.
Press on; the trumpet sounded.
"Press on," the Master cries.
"March on! March on to victory!
For victory is My cry!"
The lights are flashing brightly, and
Signals are loud and clear.
Move on, move on to victory!
Move on, for He is near.

Learning to Love

As I begin to pray, I learn to love
And devote my affections to the Lord up above.
Asking His guidance
And being led by His hand, denying myself
As I center my life around His plan.
Wanting only to do His will
As I give away my life
That another life I might fulfill.

Realization

Realizing Christ is mine sometimes is hard to do.
Fears and doubts cause many tears by
Keeping His truth from shining through.
Nevertheless, Christ still is mine.
It is a fact that can't be changed.
He gave His all to cleanse our hearts,
And willingly, He took the blame

Faith

"Just have faith," you've heard it said.
It is true; just believe.
We must have faith that all was paid,
And He is standing very near.
For faith in God will bring us out
When all else has been tried and failed.
Throw all your cares upon Him;
Believe He cares for you.
Eternal life He offers to you so
Free and clear.
Faith in God is the
Only price that before us that appears as we
Trust in him and follow very near.

Joy

Joy that is unspeakable and
Joy unheard of.
Joy among the living;
Its voice shall be heard.

To Become as Little Children

Asking us to become as little
Children
Is a strange saying, indeed!
Children do trust their parents,
Why can't we
Trust our
Heavenly Father and
Take firmly hold of His hand
For we need to be led while living
On this land?

My Little Light

My little, little light isn't very bright.
To show others the way,
I must work with all my might.
I may not accomplish what you can do,
But I must keep my little light
Trimmed and true.
God has left it in my confidence
And my care.
He knows my abilities and burdens to bear.
This earth's darkness
Can't smother out my little light
For God has ordained it to shine
Throughout the night.

The Hand that Leads

Hold steady to the hand that leads the way.
Hold steady; we have only to listen to obey.
Not by thunder and lightning
Will you hear His voice.
Just listen to the still, small plea,
And make Him your choice.

Giving to Others

Giving to others will be the
Motto if we are to find satisfaction.
Christmastime leaves such a
Wonderful, warm feeling as we
Are giving of ourselves.
We take time to give a smile, a
Hello, and hold the door open for a stranger.
We say thank you, and may even
Telephone a friend we haven't
Seen for a long time.

Giving is such a great feeling,
So why don't we do it all the time?
Sometimes Jesus had to go and rest,
But only for a season.
He was right back, giving.
Our life is in giving; there isn't
Any other way.
We can try everything else, and we
Will never find happiness until we
Start giving.

We are so tuned in to our own thinking.
That we can shut our eyes to others' needs.
The sad part of it all is the more
We get, the more we want.
We have that insatiable feeling
As we hoard unto ourselves.

We open the channels,
And the shackles fall off
When we are open to life.
I believe charity begins at home,
But before long, it will spread out
All around us as love cannot be
Contained.
We know all too well how to take.
We do not know how to give.
We can give comfort,
Understanding, a smile, and spread
Peace and good cheer.
Another word for God is "giving."
If we love, we will give.

What impresses you most about a
Person is whether he or she is a giver
Or a taker.
We must have love to live,
Even if we need to give it to ourselves.
It is the source of life.
We are our brother's keeper.
We are servants to our fellow humans.

Hope in Someone

Hope in someone you cannot see?
I cannot do it; it's beyond me.
No one understands; no one cares.
I'm left here to die.
"Oh, dear God, hear my cry!"
Wait! Why did I say "God"?
There must be a little hope dwelling within.
For if there is a God, and He doesn't change,
Maybe, just maybe, this load He will lift.
For my days are numbered and are well spent.

Yet, as I look around me,
There is someone much worse than I.
Forgive me, dear Lord, answer my cry.
I believe I can carry this load of mine.
Please, just lift my friend,
Who seems to be bending lower,
Much lower than I have been.

Searching

Search for truth until truth is found.
Truth can be shadowed by fear.
Who will dare be strong?
Who will slay the dragon
As it puffs out the smoke of envy,
Not willing to let anyone pass its borders?
When met face-to-face, the dragon
Is only puffing.
There is nothing behind its ugly threats.

Who will dare venture out to sea?
Only a few!
Searching, who will lead?
Who will clear the way?
Who will seek the truth until his
Sweat becomes as droplets?
Who will tear down the wall of vengeance?
The walls of our imagination
Only need to be confronted to see them crumble.
The foundations were not made of concrete;
They were decayed mortar.
Truth shall stand, lead, and guide.
There is great wealth in the
Depths, in the heights, and
Just beyond our grasp, out of the
Reach of the ordinary.

Treasures can only be found by searching.
Treasures of wisdom are very precious.
The discard floats down the
Stream ... easy to find.
But what have we?
Shall we be content with the
Leftovers?
Go against the current;
Use our resources,
Reinforce our ideas, and
Reevaluate our intentions.
Will we ever be satisfied with the
Discard?
Or will we be found paddling
Upstream for the treasures?

One Hope

I have only one hope, one aim—
To spread good tidings of great
Joy to my people
As they come to me.

My Will

Perfect peace comes
When you know my will.
My will is that you be in health and prosper,
Even as your soul prospers.

My Salvation Is Free

Peace I give unto you!
My salvation is free!
Why struggle within and without,
And terrified be?
Anxieties and unbelief can only torment.
That is why God, His Son has sent.
Move on, move into that heavenly rest.
No harm can befall you.
I have prepared for you the best.
No, money cannot buy it for it is
Not for sale. If peace could be bought,
It would only fail. All this world
Shall vanish away
So move on into my mansion
I have prepared for you today.

Holding You

My mercy shall hold you.
Don't ever doubt.
My mercy shall hold you.
My love you shall see.
My mercy shall hold you.
You have only to believe!

Boredom

Boredom only results from not
Doing the duty at hand.
Do what you know to do, and then
When you are finished,
Time will take care of itself.
We sometimes eat, trying to take
Away that gnawing inside us
That comes from not doing what
We know to do.

Satisfaction

Satisfaction in our vocation is
Worth striving to attain.
Only then can we be truly contented.
Dissatisfaction is sometimes discouraged,
But it should never be discouraged.
When dissatisfaction is used
As a stepping stone,
Great avenues can emerge to open
New doors.

The Crowd

We can be brainwashed by the crowd.
We should look at
The crowd before conforming.
Their hang-ups may be even
Greater than our own.

Vain Thoughts

Keep your head.
Do not be disillusioned by vain thoughts
Puffing you up, only to let you down.
Truth will hold you steady and
Can never let you down.

My Friend

Who stayed in the garden all alone that night?
Who's sweat was like droplets of blood
While waiting for the answer to
Come into sight?
Who said, "Not my will, but
Thine be done" (Luke 22:42 KJV)?
That was Jesus, who died not in vain.
Who will always lead you;
Hold His hand.
Who will comfort us if
Friends fail?
Who will forgive you if unbelief does abound?
That is Jesus, who died not in vain.
Who came to earth in a bundle of love?
Who walked with us,
Showing forth His love?
Who had compassion when no one cared?
That was Jesus, my Savior and friend!

My Words Are Life

I see those tormenting thoughts.
Those thoughts came not from me.
They come to rob you of your hope.
I gave you that hope.
Remember, my words are spirit.
My words are life.

A Higher Power

"Come up higher unto Me."
There is a higher power in each of us.
We have only to listen and
Arise, and find peace!
What God has for us is beyond
Measure.

I Love You, I Love You

I love you, I love you.
I heard ringing throughout the night.
I love you, I love you.
Don't give up the fight.
We can fight to keep faith among
Our doubts and fears.
We can fight to smile when
Sorrow creeps near.
Remember, I'm the one
Loving you when I hold you, my dear.

Sent

Jesus was sent to the hungry, poor,
Wretched, and blind.
Sent to the feeble, deserted, the
One left behind.
He was sent to bring peace in
Our times of strife.
He was sent to bring good tidings
Of a new life.
"Yes, you are sent,"
God Himself has said.
"Sent, yes, now go for you are sent!
As my messenger, go.
As my peace, you must go.
Go for today
My love you can sow.
Go for the world to see!
Go for tomorrow holds for thee.
Go, my beloved, go in Me."

Let No One Take Your Crown

Hold fast to whatever you have.
Let no one take your crown.
Endure until the end for a reward
Shall abound.
A cross we gladly bear until the
Crown we see
For God's grace is enough.
We have only to believe.

Fully Redeemed

Fully redeemed, brought back to God.
Fully redeemed, for a long time I have sought
Complete redemption and nothing
Between me and my Maker as
He washes me pure and clean.
God's grace is enough for all my needs.
When my strength has collapsed
He then intercedes.
He keeps me afloat, not letting me to sink.
Proving me as gold tried in the fire,
I have only to believe.

Calm My Fears

Please, Jesus, calm my fears that
Are raging high.
Take away my doubts; please hear my cry.
Help me to grasp that You come to give life.
You come to give peace among my strife.
To all who will hear, listen, and obey,
God comes to lift the load and
Give courage this day.
He comes to give peace to the tormented soul.
He comes to give courage to make
Us bold.
He gives strength for weakness
That plagues our minds.
God comes to loosen our spirits
From the shackles that bind.
Think on things that are holy and pure.
Love and mercy will always endure.
Faith and trust will never fail.
If God can save, He can heal.

My God Lives

My God lives.
He lives within my heart.
My God lives, and
His love He shall impart.
He lives for the world to see.
My God He lives.
He lives for you and me.
My God He lives.
He lives today.
My God He lives.
He lives to show the way.

Direct Me

Dear God,
Direct me today—
Each thing I do, each word I say—
So that when this day is passed and gone,
I can rest assured
That Your will was done.
Renew within me a right spirit this
Day, oh, Lord.
Forgive all hatred, envy, and strife.
Take away all and give me newness of life.
You can see the terror and
Torment in my mind.
Come today, and open my eyes
That are blind.
They are so blind that I cannot see.
Make the way clear.
Lord, make the way clear to me.
You know of my distress, doubt, and fear.
Dear God, help me as you have in the past?.
Dear God, I give You all of me at last.

My People, Come Eat

My people, come eat of My corn
And drink of My wine.
Come eat; come and dine.
There is meat for the hungry.
There is corn for the weak.
There's food aplenty.
Come, please, come seek.
Minds shall be opened.
Deaf ears unstopped.
Come now, there's mercy
Flowing over the top.

Show Me the Way

The heart reaches out, but the
Mind can't see.
There is a need of rest;
Rest in Thee.
Turmoil, confusion, and terror—
Oh, please!
Show me the way; I cannot see.
My heart cries out; there is hope,
And there is peace.
I cannot find it; show me, please!
Help me! Help me!
Is there no hope for me?
I thought You came to give life?
I haven't found it yet among the
Envy and strife.
I'm sinking deep; the darkness encloses.
Why try? There isn't anyone who cares.
Living or dying, it is torment I share.
Who's calling and tugging at me now?
Stop! Don't pull me back; this is my hour.
Whose hand is that taking hold of mine?
I've been lifted and let down too many times.
This hand is different—firm, steady, and strong!
Could it be my heart was wrong?
It's true, it's true when the light breaks through.
When the clouds are dark, and the sky is blue,
There is a God who cares. My heart was true.

Waiting at My Feet

Peace I give, to all who'll rest in My arms today.
Peace, I give in a world of hate.
Peace I give; all I ask is wait.
Waiting at my feet, look fully in My face.
Waiting at my feet, all fear I shall erase.

King of Kings

He has spanned the tide between God and humankind.
That's Jesus, the crucified.
He hath repaired the breach so all can live.
That's Jesus, the resurrected.
He has given all power to humankind.
That's Jesus, the Kings of Kings.

It Is You I Adore

Thank You, Jesus, for breath today
To whisper, "I love You," from these
Lips of clay.
The sweetest peace settles over my soul
When I whisper, "I love You. It's You
I adore."

Believe! Believe!

His hands and feet
Were nailed for you.
His heart so heavy and tired is true.
His body, wrecked by sin and shame,
Arise, arise in Jesus's name!
There's a fountain flowing deep and wide.
Abundant life is swelling with the tide.
Believe! Believe! Step out and
Claim your healing now
In Jesus's name.

Victory

We are created in the image of our Father.
We are given the love He shared
With His Son.
Striving to bring us all together,
The victory has already been won.
Salvation was all provided, and
Healing completed too.
Believe! The work is finished.
Believe! Believe!
There's nothing left to do.
Faith … He gave us our portion.
Using it is our duty now.
Build upon the solid foundation,
One that evil can't tear down.

I Am the Lord, Thy God

I heard you whispering,
"I am the Lord, thy God,"
It dawned on me;
I was a child of the King!
My Father, the Maker of all
Living things.
Oh, how my heart sings.
I am born into the royal family,
And that makes me free.
My Father loves His children,
So happy are we.

Confidence

Where have you placed your confidence today?
If in the things you possess, it can melt away.
Confidence in the Lord, our God,
Our thoughts dwelling on Him,
Will be enough while on this earth
And will prove worthwhile in the end.

Our Consciences

Our consciences play a big part in our lives.
Guard it; keep it clear
If you are wise.
Obedience to God will keep it right.
Boldness, faith, and confidence
Will be our might.
Condemnation will rob us of
Faith in God,
Watch the path you dare to trod.
With a sensitive conscience
Centered on His trust,
Determined to obey, obey we must.

Road Signs

The path is straight.
The road signs clearly marked.
Grave attention must be paid, and
Every signal harked.
For there are detour signs
Posted along the way,
Reading there is a shorter route.
But no attention pay.

If you should be snared
By one of these signs,
You'll notice all your joy
You left behind.
Oh, where is my joy?
You have a soul
Longing for its Maker.
The detour road is indeed a faker.

On this road you will notice, too,
There is excitement only for a season.
Then you are left lonely, sad, and blue.
Read the road map, and study it carefully.
A mansion awaits you, so travel prayerfully.
Roadblocks also intervene along our way;
Stopping for a season shall be our dismay.

But wait on God; don't detour at all.
Remember, patience will win out.
God won't let you fall.
As we keep our eyes on the gate called Strait,
Pressing ahead to that future date when all the
Stumbling blocks laid in our way,
Will long be forgotten.
Oh! What a glorious day

Walking and Talking with Jesus

Walking with Jesus
Each day of my life.
There's nothing sweeter, no envy, no strife.
Talking with Jesus and taking
Hold of His hand
As I offer Him my life to fulfill His plan.
His plan is indeed the perfect way,
Shaped and molded day after day.
The glorious good, alongside the bad,
Knowing someday only the good
I shall have.

By praying and seeking, His plan
Is made clear.
Dwelling in the Spirit
I have love … no fear.
Complete trust He offers
On wings of prayer.
Faith, hope, deliverance,
All three are there.

We can Conquer Fear

1. We Can Conquer Fear

We can stop fear at the door
When we guard our minds.
Fear is an emotion that will
Bind, hamper, and keep us in
Bondage.

We lose our courage.
We are not free to do and act
As we wish to do.
We also can have a fear of
Failure.

Fear can cause us to feel less
Than a healthy person.
Fear can be real.
Fear can be imaginary.
We can usually deal with our real fears.

It is the imaginary fears that
Keep us in bondage.
Letting our mind dwell on
Things that might happen is
Where the harm lies.
We cannot live a full life with
Fear of what might happen
When we stop and confront
Our fears.

Fear is our worst enemy.
We give that fear life, and it
Takes control.

We can allow fear to strain,
Tighten, and destroy all
Confidence.

We cannot think, eat, sleep, or
Rest.
We torture ourselves.
Our fears are not going to keep
Danger away.
We give fear so much life that
It appears to be bigger than we
Are.
It can be overwhelming.
Fearing something that may
Not happen throws us into
Torment.

The chains of fear are real as
Long as we allow those fears
To be real and to overshadow
The truth.
Fear can destroy both soul
And body.

When fear is brought to the
Light, darkness is no longer
Present.
Peace and trust will give us
Confidence
To act against that danger
When it does appear.

We can face our fears.
Our words of truth will cause
Those fears to flee.
God does not give us a spirit of
Fear but a sound mind.

Being bound by fear is
Truly not a sound mind.
We can quote words to that fear, and
It will flee out of our thinking.
Remember, God does
Not give us the spirit of fear
But of love, power, and a
Sound mind.

We can love ourselves so
Much that we won't let
Torment enter our thinking.
We have that power.
We have only to exercise that
Kind of thinking.

Love is greater than fear.
God gave us His Spirit to
Overcome those thoughts that
Take away our peace.
We may have to quote those
Words of life several times.
Torment will flee as we think
About trust, peace, love, and
God's care.
Being thankful for all the times
God has protected us with
His love
Will help us receive the comfort for us now.
If we let love be our motivator …
Fear will not be our conqueror.

Fear is like a staph infection,
Spreading from one victim to
Another until many are
Infected.

Trust and faith are uplifting, giving
A feeling of worth, not degradation.

Godliness is complete trust.

You have only to listen to
God's voice to receive
Understanding, wisdom,
And peace.

Truth leads upward and
Forward at the same time.

2. Face-to-Face

I see the Master face-to-face.
I wrote in one of the poems,
"When all can see My face in you,
Then they will know you are
True.
Just to see the Master face-to-
Face,
All our cares will be erased."

"When at the throne I humbly bow,
I hear Him say, 'this is your hour.'
"Just to see the Master in all His glory
Shall be my hope, my faith, and
My story."

Perseverance seems to be the
Key to finding oneself.

3. Reservations

At first you may have all
Manner of reservations
Concerning My love.
My love
Is so gentle it has been overlooked,
Trod upon, and cast down.
Since I am love,
I will arise and overcome
And prevail over all.
Failures and disappointments
May come.
Remember those who endure
Until the end
Receive their deliverance.
Your mind did not get in this
Shape overnight.
There is hope that won't fail;
Little by little, precept upon
Precept, line upon line,
Until the walls of fear crumble,
With faith taking hold.

4. God, What Can I Do?

If you wonder what God wants
You to do,
Do what you know to do.
When you are finished,
You will have insight to do
More.

Don't let fear hold you back.
When confronted,
Fear is usually imaginary.
Be not afraid to live.
In living you will find life.
You have one life to give.
May you never let fear
Hamper your giving.

5. Contentment

Contentment—oh, so hard to
Find!
Where is it hiding?

Contentment!
I don't believe true
Contentment comes from
Attaining a goal.

We often interpret that as
Contentment.
I truly believe contentment is
Giving of oneself completely.
The act of giving renders true
Contentment.
We are a vessel, flowing in and
Out to others.

We are the most depressed
When we are not giving
Either by word or deed.
Giving seems to be life's secret.
As we give, we become
Richer by the experience.

6. Try

We learn by our past
Experiences.
Even though failure may come,
We are better for have tried.

We have gained knowledge
That we could not have
Learned any other way.
Success comes from real concern.
If we would be successful,
We need to search out every
Opportunity that comes our way.
Do not fear to be yourself;
There is only one you.

7. Every Eye Shall Behold Him

What kind of a portrait does our
Daily lives portray of God?
Do they do Him justice?
Do our lives reflect
A baby in a manger,
A child teaching in the Temple,
A young man working as a carpenter,
A healer of the sick and
Oppressed?
We can let those who are
Bound go free as we take
Away their confusion, doubts,
And fears,
Giving confidence that God
Lives.
We can point the way for others
To find peace for themselves.

8. Forgiveness

We freely give
When we forgive.
We are seeing our fellow humans
As ourselves.
Forgiving is love in action.

Do not fear to live.
Only by living will we find life.

Detours can be used to chart a better
Course.

I have only one life to give.
May I never let fear hamper
My giving.

9. Born of God

My wish is for everyone to
Know they are children of God.
The only sin we acquire at
Birth is fear.

Fear is here!
Fear keeps us from
Believing that we are
His children.

How can we be so intelligent
And not
Know we are Your children?
If we would cast our cares on Thee,
Then pray, "Have Thy will in me."
Remembering the prayer and
Believing for the best,
We would have peace and perfect rest.

10. Peace

You say I can find peace in
The storms of life.

Peace during all this
Trouble and strife.

Peace, oh,
Where can it be found?
I have looked and looked;
There isn't any around.
There must be a brighter day.
I'm still going to hope.
Maybe, if He opens my eyes
That I can see
There is someone who needs
Even me.

I can't do much; my life is far spent.
I'll reach out my hand and try to find peace,
By helping those He has sent.

11. The Gift of God

The precious baby born on Christmas day
Was really God's love
Bundled up and sent our way.

His love didn't start in the
Manger that night.
His love started when the
World was flung into sight.
He loved us so much that in
His image we were made.
God was not selfish when He
Made this body of clay.
God cares so much that
Lonesome, He didn't want us
To be.

Our every desire
He wishes to intercede.
In the garden of Eden was
Enduring love.
Then when man failed, God
Provided a place up above.

His love … is determination
That never gives up when we fail.
For down through the ages,
His love hath prevailed.
"Peace on Earth, and Goodwill
To all Men" (Luke 2:14 KJV),

Was love ringing clear to all
Tired of sin.
God's love is that force that
Speaks to our hearts,
That pleads there is a better
Way: "My peace I can impart."

Love is the fulfillment of the
Law.
Love drives out fear and
Cushions our every fall.

We complicate the message,
Making a mystery out of God's
Word when Jesus Christ and His
Love still needs to be heard.

12. Answer the Call

Why do we hold back and
Do not give our all?
Great blessings await us
When we answer the call.

13. Launch Out

We must get out into deep
Waters to swim.
For if we start to sink,
On Him we will depend.
If we stay along the shore,
We will rely on our abilities
More and more.

14. Finding Peace

We only need to seek peace to
Find it!
We only need to knock on the
Door of peace,
And that door will open.
We only need to lay aside
Fear
To listen to the still small
Voice
Dwelling within, waiting to be
Heard.

Everything else will fail us.
We are complete within.
We need not listen to another
Voice.
We have the necessary tools to
Find peace.

When we have found peace,
We then can lend a helping
Hand
To those who are steeped in
Bondage.

We can hasten their escape
From negative thinking.
The warfare is in our minds.
Our thinking is the firing line,
The front line of battle.
When we choose to have peace,
We will find peace.

15. Thinking

Thinking is a word
Not much used today.
Thinking will bring us back
When we start to stray.
Thinking can bring fear or
Peace of mind.
On what we think
Makes the difference
We will find.

16. Alone

The road may seem lonely,
Dark with fear.
Remember, there is still
Someone who is standing near.

Near to the One who wants to
Share
Our grief and pain.
So please, don't despair!

If there is life, there is
Hope.
Hope in God, a friend so true.
Hope in God will see us through,
Through the long nights and
Empty days.
There must be something for
Us to give praise!

Maybe our eyes are growing
Dim, but if there is still a little
Light, be thankful to Him.
He cares; we have only to believe.
He is our Savior and Healer indeed.

17. Satisfied

Sometimes we're haughty,
High-minded, and rude.
Our souls aren't satisfied
With this earthly food.

We must have food
From above
Daily to live;
Give me His love.

Our souls grope
In the dark,
Trying to see
And failing to hark.

We must have food
From above
Daily to live;
Give me His love.

Food for morning,
Food for night.
My soul cries out!
Give me sight.

We must have food
From above
Daily to live;
Give me His love.

18. I, Too, Found Him in a Manger

While searching for God,
I was dazzled by the
Brightness of the stars.
The swaddling clothes of my
Mind
Concealed His identity.

The lowly One, the humble birth,
A child in a manger instead of the inn.
My soul desired His fellowship.
I was sure God was
In the traditions, rites, and rituals.

I did not find Him there.
After exhausting my efforts,
Suddenly God appeared!
He had been there all the
Time, waiting patiently,
Knowing I would return.
Finding out the truth was where
My peace lay when all had failed.
He, being the pearl of great price,
Was standing with open arms,
Not the least bit angry.
Only kind and gentle,
Ready to receive me,
Thus, becoming the King of Kings.

We cannot go anywhere idling.
We need to get into gear.

We do not listen.
Therefore, we do not learn.
Fear is blinding. Faith brings sight.

19. Dream

We can dream; we must dream.
We also must make that dream
A reality.

We can pray; we can raise our faith.
We must put legs to our prayers.

This is a beautiful formula,
A stirring, moving observation.

Expending our energy into action
To make the heritage
We leave a workable force

20. Declaration of Our Spirit to Lead and to Guide Us

I am peace.
I do not punish.
Think and speak positively,
And you can deliver yourself and
Help those around you.

Don't parade your faith.
Let that faith do a work in you.
Then it will shine unto others.

My love,
Don't base your happiness
On what others think.
Be true to yourself.
Know your worth.

I have set before you
Life and death.
Choose which you will serve:
Peace or torment,
Faith or doubt.
Your mind can drive nails
Into your hands and feet,
Place the thorns
Upon your head, and
Pierce your side with a staff.
Your mind can also be the angel

That rolls away the stone,
Letting you find peace within
Yourself.
At times you are crucified.
At times you are resurrected.
Each time, new life breaks forth.

Shake fear that is hiding in your mind.
You shall receive new life.
My love will heal all
Dis-eases of the mind.
I have only one hope, one aim—
To spread good tidings of great
Joy to my people on land,
On the sea, and in the air.

Perfect peace comes when you
Know my will.
My will is that you be in health
And prosper
As you free yourself of fear and doubt.
Traditions have my people
Bound hand and foot.
I did not set those boundaries.
They do not believe in a living Savior,
A Savior who lives within.
I see my people clearly.
They are a people without a Shepherd.
Not satisfied, going here and there,
Believing what others tell them.

You do not listen to your spirits'
Small voice.
The voice that dwells within to
Lead and to guide you to all
Truth.

Come up higher unto me.
There is a higher power dwelling
Within.
You have only to listen.
Arise! And find peace.

What I have for you is beyond measure.
I want this nation to flourish
And become a healthy nation.
A nation that is undivided and free
From partiality.
I wish only good
For those who seek good.
No, you will not enjoy the roses
Without the thorns,
But you will appreciate the
Beauty.

There is a workable force in your
Life, waiting to be turned loose.
Speak the truth to your neighbor.
Learn from each other.

I come to give life, strength, and
Peace instead of punishment.
I speak life to you.
I want you to have life more abundant.

I do not want you to have a
Life that is cramped,
Hampered, or bound.
I have only the best for you.
Rest again, I say; let your mind
Rest.
Even as I speak to you this day,
You will find rest.
There shall be a peace flow over
You.
You shall find rest, peace, and
Comfort.

Love yourself as I love you.
Torment shall you drive out.
Fear shall have to leave.
Be good to yourself.
You will know how to
Free your fellow persons.

The key to a happy life is finding
Out the truth.
The truth will open the closed
Door of your mind and
Free your soul.
Your mind can have your soul in
Bondage.

My knowledge is worth seeking.
Satisfaction and fulfillment can be
Attained.
You need not be discouraged.

There is something you can do
That is fulfilling.
I see the pressures
This way and that way, no time to be
You.
Wait, who are you?
Have you discovered who you are?
What are your ambitions?
Taking time to evaluate your priorities
Can prove to be enriching.

21. God's Words of Love

Will hold you,
Will be near you
To comfort you,
Guide you,
Live with you,
Dwell within,
Make you whole,
Diminish your fears,
Work out your problems,
Share your grief,
Feel your pain,
Move those mountains,
Rid you of hate,
Take away your pride,
Lift you up from degradation,
Give you liberty,
Rid you of spite,
Cast out evil imaginations,
Give life,
Take away your suffering.

22. God's Word Will:

Show us a better way,
Whisper sweet words of wisdom,
Lift your faith,
Put down frustrations,
Calm the storms,
Hold your hand,
Deliver you from your enemies,
Make a way for your escape,
Hold you when all else fails.

23. God's Inheritance for His Children

My joy is contagious.
My victory is won.
I have been with you
Before you were born.
You know not My visitation.
My existence has no earthly origin;
I am Spirit.
I dwell within.
I am implanted in life.
I am life.

Let Me be.
I feel what you feel.
How do I feel what you feel?
I dwell within.
When you hurt, I hurt.
When you bleed, I bleed.
When your heart aches, mine aches.
When you rejoice, I rejoice.
When you have faith, we join forces.
How can you fail? I am with you.

I am your friend.
I fail not.
What might be a failure
Is only a stepping-stone
To something better.

Pick up the pieces, and
Put them back together.
Look for life, and you shall find it.
You were born with a measure of faith.
Let that seed be born in you.
Nourish that life.
Let it blossom and come
Forth to full stature.
I am life.
I am peace.
I am wisdom.
I am whatever you need.
Stop condemning yourself.
I do not condemn you.
I know how you feel.
I understand you.

The sun is shining upon this
Nation
With peace, love, and mercy.
I will lead my people out of bondage.
My love will lift your mind
As you go forth this day
To heights and depths unknown.

Peace shall be yours, like a river.
Peace amid the storms of life.
Peace from all envy,
Hatred, and strife.
Peace, peace in the night.

I come to make a way
Where there is no way.
I see a way being made in the
Desert,
In the valley of defeat, and in
Indecisions.
I see a way being made; look up.
There is hope, never doubt.
Faith will win out over all.
I love My people.
I would not that they perish.
I would not that they be
Tormented.

I would that they have life
More abundant.
There is life amid
The thorns and thistles.
There is life in challenges you will see.
There is life; push on, only believe.

When you see yourself,
You shall see Me.

Life is yours this day.
Take it please.
Even though the load seems
Greater than you can bear,
Hold on! Just one more mile, and
You will find a way.

I see the thoughts that come
Against you.
Those thoughts are not of Me.
They come to rob you of hope.
I give you hope.
I give you strength to press
Through, even unto the other side.
Remember, My words are Spirit.
My words are truth.

You are My concern.
I watch over you day and night.
I know your fears, and
I see your weaknesses.
I have faith in you.
I encourage and believe in you.
I have given you power.

Use that strength to free yourself
And to free your fellow people.
Face life with courage.
Ask for wisdom to meet your
Needs.
Listen to My voice;
Pursue with confidence.

Rushing waters, thunder, and
Lightning,
Crashing and beating upon your
Life.
Be still, knowing there is a way.

You have only to seek to find the
Way.
Don't tune Me out.
I am your friend.
I'm on your side.
I'll fight for you.
I'll be there to comfort and
See you through.

I will not withhold good from you.
I want for you the best.
Wishful thinking
Should never take the place
Of getting a job done.

Chart your course, and
Follow with all your might.
Be at peace with yourself.
Know that I dwell within
To lead and to guide you.
Pursue those talents that you
Possess.
Push through your fears, and
Erase those doubts.
Dare to step out because each
Challenge
Can be a rewarding adventure.

Mountains, I see those mountains!
Insurmountable, you say.

Take that mountain apart piece by piece.
You will see that mountain
Disappear
In front of your eyes.

You can do whatever you desire to
Do.
Only believe that all things are possible.
I see those mountains moving.
Yes, they are moving out of your
Way.

I am the God of mercy.
I make a way where there is no
Way.
Just believe I come to make a way for
You.
I have mercy to give.
I give you love, peace, and
Understanding.
Condemnation shall vanish.

Guilt shall have to flee
For My love shall overshadow all
Evil that looms so great.
Evil that could drown you.
My love is greater.
I would that you have life and
That you have peace in your heart
And in your soul.

Wisdom is yours; take it please!
I'm handing it to you.
Take it please! It's yours; it's your
Heritage.
I see the unrest, the tossing and
Turning,
The unsatisfied feeling, and the
Emptiness.
I did not promise you a bed of
Roses.
I did promise you strength to meet
Each need and
Courage to open every door,
And faith to meet each challenge.
Are you weary today?

Take it easy; be good to yourself.
I want you to be good to yourself.
I don't want any harm to befall
You
For you are a pearl of great price.

I see that cloak of fear
That keeps My light
From shining
In the darkness
To free your mind.
Be not dismayed.
My light shall break through
Every barrier that is raised against
You.
My peace is your peace.

My understanding is your
Understanding.
Your insides cry out to be
Delivered.

Your mind is in bondage.
It will not believe that I dwell within.
Your mind will not believe
I am the Lord thy God,
That I care for you, and
I will not let you perish.
Believe, only believe!

I was with you from the
Beginning.
I shall be with you to the end.
Search for truth.
Don't be content until you find it.
My truth shall be life unto you.
I am life.
I care about you.
I want the best for you.
I have prepared the best for you.
Don't be content
Until all fear is gone.
Then you shall be free.
I see those struggles, struggles unending.
You can't see the end of struggles.

Be not weary. Without challenges,
You would never know your
Strength.
You are stronger than you believe you
Are.

You are a strong people.
A mighty nation.
Arise above your fears, and
Confront your struggles
Using courage and fortitude.

You shall always have gentleness
And support from My loving arms.
Warmth, tenderness, and caring are
Yours.
You deserve the best.
You have stood the test.
Be not weary in well-doing.
You shall surely receive the
Profits.
What you give shall return to you.

There is rest in My arms this day—
Peace, rest, and comfort.
Be not dismayed; keep searching.
My truth shall set you free.
Give that which I have given you.
It shall be food for another.

Rest and contentment shall be yours
When my life flows through you
Unto others.
Grace and truth can be compared
To a rose in full bloom,
A scene that is breathtaking and glorious.

24. The Greatest Story of Love

The greatest love story known
To humankind
Is the waiting and wooing
For my love in each life.
Bringing out the best, never condemning,
Only lifting, guiding, and knowing
You will return when you have
Exhausted all your efforts in finding peace.

My love never rushes but
Gently leads and guides with a
Steady hand.
I suffer when you suffer.
I rejoice when you rejoice.
I am ever understanding and ready
To rescue my people.
I come to set my people free and
To let them know that I dwell
Within.

25. Partiality

Partiality is not known in me.
I am life unto all.
I come to lead you out of bondage.
I come to fulfill your life.
I come to free your thinking; I come to
Take away strife.
My peace is flowing like a river.
My peace is free, pure, and strong.
My peace sweeps over your soul and
Into the unknown. Don't be afraid;
Fear not!

You have heard me say before,
"Fear not! Only believe!"
Please know I do not fail.
Fear not, and peace shall prevail.
Love and mercy are yours.
Peace and contentment are yours.
You have paid the price,
The price of letting me become
Your friend and your guide.
There is peace in the raging
Waters.
There is peace during torment.
There is peace for I make all things
Well.

Pride comes before a fall.

Confidence in God is strength.

Embracing Our Spirit Is The Essence of Life

We honor the Creator when we honor ourselves. We learn to love ourselves as much as God loves us.

Embracing Our Spirit

Listen to our spirit.
Nurture our spirit.
Getting the nurturing we didn't receive as a child.

Everyone needs to be validated. If we were not validated as a child, it is not too late. We can blame someone else for where we are today. We cannot blame someone else where we will be tomorrow. We can validate ourselves and be a whole, healthy people.

We can only help ourselves ...
Others can give information, instructions, and directions. We make the decisions in our lives! We have the final say! We can nourish ourselves. We can love ourselves enough to change our way of thinking.

The negative recordings going around and around in our head can be stopped, never to be an influence again. We are the captains of our ships. We are the pilots of our planes. We are the creators of our destinies. We can rely on our faith.

It all starts with encouragement and loving oneself as to speak kind and loving words to be a healthy, happy person. Rely on God to give us wisdom.

You are the greatest person you know. Honor yourself. Listen to what you have to say. You will find it is important, and you will learn to be true to yourself, to love yourself, and to be thankful you are who you are.

No one on this earth is like you.
No one else thinks as you think.
No one else has the words that you have to say.
No one else loves as you love.
No one else cares as you care.
No one has felt what you have felt, learned what you have learned, and lives as you live.
We honor the Creator when we honor ourselves.

1. What Is Our Spirit?

Our spirit has a voice, and we are listening to that voice whether we realize it as our spirit or not. If the Spirit is something that seems too far out to understand, hopefully when you finish this book, you will know with a surety that your spirit is not a mystery. Our spirit is to be protected and cherished. Our spirit is the source of life … it is life.

Words can lift our spirit, or words can kill our spirit.
Words are very powerful. The results of words affect our spirit. Thoughts are words when spoken. Thoughts can kill our spirit, or thoughts can lift our spirit. We are what we think. Our mind is the door to our spirit. What we think determines how we feel.

I was reared in a very religious home. The preachers taught fear as a conqueror. You do not do this or that, or God will not let you go to heaven. We were controlled by fear. Fear was not satisfying my need deep within. I began to see that I was born with that same spirit of love. Love, not fear, is to be our motivator. It is love that will see us through any obstacle. If we allow fear to lead and guide us, it will fail us when we need it most.

Fear binds, grips, shackles, and destroys every good thought that we have. Fear does not open doors. It always shuts the doors before we get a chance to enter.

Fear can nip every thought or action in the bud before it matures. As I said earlier, the mind is the door to your spirit. When your mind entertains fear, fear grips your spirit.

I wrote a poem with the following lines: "Take heed on what your mind and spirit feed. What you think about makes a difference you will find." Maybe you have had hopes and dreams, and you told a friend. Your friend may have disagreed, and you let what he or she thought stop those dreams. Your spirit was killed. You let someone else take control of your most precious possession, your spirit. We need to put a guard on our spirit. That friend disagreeing with your dreams and ambitions expressed his or her opinion, not yours. You were following that person's spirit. You need to think of your spirit as the key to your happiness. A gut feeling can be a direct guiding of our spirit. Instead of believing your spirit, you tell yourself, "My friend was probably right." You never opened the door to your dreams.

Our spirit is to lead and guide us. To be tuned in to our spirit is the most precious gift we can give ourselves. Our spirit wants only what is best for us. Our spirit looks out for our good. Our spirit will lead and guide us if we believe it is on our side.
We can reprogram our thinking. Refuse to think on thoughts that are not for our good. We can stop the recording in our thinking that is negative and works against us being our best self.

We cannot help how we were taught in the past, but we can control what we believe today and tomorrow.
If those thoughts in the past kept doors slamming in our face, we are now in control of those thoughts. We are born a child of love. Just as sure as we let fear conquer us, we can now let love be the motivator. No one else can have that control unless we give them that power.

When our intentions are for good, our spirit is free to lead and guide. We start working for our good. We start being our best friend. We start to love, keeping a guard on our spirit. We like feeling good. Not that we will not feel bad again. There will be times when we will be hurt.

We cannot control what people say or do, and we will not understand why we are being hurt. But we can control how we let it affect our spirit—how we think and feel. We do have control over that. It took me a while to learn this truth.

This truth has helped me through many trials. It has never failed to see me through difficult times. This truth will never fail!

Love leaves a feeling of hope, trust, and faith. As we think on love and caring for ourselves, our spirit is lifted. We feel good. We have a true outlook on life. We have faith that we can accomplish whatever we desire. When our mind and spirit are in harmony, then our body is free from stress. Our mind and spirit become as one. We are working for our good. When our vessel is full, we can help others.

As a child, I would hear preachers talk of the spirit. They never told us what it was. The spirit was only for certain people. We put these people on pedestals by belittling ourselves when we are all God's children. We are all born with that measure of faith. The same spirit of life breathed into us. Our spirit breathes words of life to us and encourages us to be all we can be. Our spirit comforts, lifts, guides, and directs our path without fear.

155

2. How Can I Find My Spirit?

We know what the spirit is, so now the challenge is listening to His voice.

Our true spirit is very gentle and comforting. We may have overridden our true spirit of love for so long that it is a habit. We are not tuned in. At first, we will not believe our spirit of truth … We think it cannot be that God loves us so much that He wants what is best for us. We may not believe that we deserve that kind of spirit comforting us no matter what. An unconditional love! Inside me! What have I done to deserve this? We were born with it. It is ours. It is our heritage.

We had nothing to do with being born with that spirit of love. It is ours. No strings attached. We can do with it as we please. That's where our thinking comes into view. There is our natural thinking, and then there is divine thinking. The scripture reads, "Think it not robbery to be equal with God" (Phil. 2:6 KJV). We have only to believe to experience that love. Jesus paid the price to show us what it is like to be a son of God.

Having God's Spirit within us does not take away from the deity of God. It really shows us His supreme nature.

My spirit soared to heights unknown when I first learned that the spirit I was born with was the spirit of love and not fear. I found that I could trust that divine spirit to lead and guide me to truth.

3. We Are Spirit

We are a spirit. Life is spirit. It is the spirit that is alive. The real spirit that we were born with is the spirit of love. When we are in the spirit of love, we are in the right Spirit. He came to show us what we really are … a child of God even as He is a child of God. The cross that He overcame was driving out the man's mind that would rule this body, which is the temple of God.

He overcame the power that would cause Him to rely on food for life.
He overcame the power that would cause him to throw himself over a cliff to tempt God to protect Him.
He overcame everything that we have to fight against today.
He overcame the rites and rituals of the church world … the Scribes and Pharisees.
He overcame their death teachings, which were death to God's Spirit being in Him.

"Greater is He that is in you than he that is in the world." (1 John 4:4 KJV). It is no different for us today than it was for Jesus when He walked this earth. The only difference is that we know Jesus was victorious, so we can be victorious also. There is no doubt about it. He overcame the human mind that sits in our thinking. It denies each thought that would suggest that we are children of God and that God dwells within the mortal body.

We conflict with God's Spirit against human thinking—Good against evil, faith against doubt, love against hate, peace against unrest, trust against unbelief. We can allow the spirit of love to grow and develop our being, thoughts, and behavior.

The mind controls the spirit, heart, and soul. That is why it is so important to be in tune with the Father of our spirit, which is the spirit of love. We will never be happy until we love ourselves enough to conquer the mind that acts against us with fear, doubt, and unbelief. Until we conquer that mind—for it is a mind-set—and substitute that mind with trust and faith that we are children of God, we will never know true contentment. We will never be one with our spirit; our house is divided, and we are in turmoil.

We are in the valley of decision; we are tormented day and night. We are striving for … we know not what. Every mind that comes against us for having the Spirit of God within us is the Antichrist (1 John 4:3 KJV). Even as in the day that Jesus walked upon this earth, they knew not his visitation. It is no different today. God is a spirit, and we are a spirit. We cannot worship Him in spirit and truth until we believe He dwells within us. His kingdom is within humankind.

4. Our Mind

Actions start in the mind. As we think, so are we. If we think it, we can do it. The mind is the center of actions. First we think, and then we do. Our mind is in control of our being. If we desire to be healthy, we have only to eat and drink the right food and get enough exercise. It is still hard even after we realize we are in control. This thing of being overcome is no mystery. It is not bigger than we are. It does not have control over us.

If we are going to have peace and be stress-free, then we are going to have to work for our own good, not against our good. We can be our own worst enemy or our own best friend. We choose … we decide what we will do for ourselves or against ourselves. Any thought that keeps us from being healthy and prosperous is our enemy. We must humble our mind. Our own thinking is against our spirit and peace.

We are limited only by the thoughts in our mind.
Our mind tells us surely it won't hurt to dwell on the negative. Surely it won't hurt this one time! You know it is against our good. Consuming the wrong food and drink is not a transgression against our soul but our body. If we want to live and enjoy our life and freedom of spirit, we must take care of our body.
As we learn to take good care of our spirit, we will learn to be kind to this body. "Seek first the kingdom of God and His righteous, then all these other things will be added unto us" (Matt. 6:33 KJV). When we seek what lifts our spirit and seek what is best for us, we will be living in harmony with our spirit. We will gain insight as to conquer all things that come against

us. Our thinking can deceive us. God's Word not only frees our spirit but frees our heart, mind, and body. God will help us to achieve our hearts' desires. Our mind controls our spirit. We can learn to keep watch over our mind.

When we find that our thinking can be our worst enemy, we can begin to awaken out of sleep. "Our ways are not God's ways." (Isa. 55:8-9 KJV). Our minds can be in bondage until we do not know what is best for our bodies. God is that Spirit of love that dwells within us … to love ourselves like God loves us and wants the best for us. We owe it to ourselves to take up for ourselves. Feelings are powers and principalities that need to be conquered when they are against what is best for us. Jesus conquered life like we must conquer life. He hid God's words within His heart.

Try to imagine how much God loves us. If we can just love ourselves a fraction as much as God loves us, we will do only what is best for ourselves. When we love ourselves, we will have peace. That is what God does; He loves us. There is no turning with God's love. There is no wavering and no doubts. We are the most precious thing that God has. That is a love we need to learn about. Learn about a love that will never fail.

When the positives start being greater than the negatives in our life, then it gets easier to do what is for our good. Some things have happened in my life, and all I could think of was the negatives. Finally, I got sick and tired of letting that rule my thinking. I decided when something negative entered my mind, I would not entertain that thought. I just said, "No, I am not going to think that way." That kind of thinking was over.

It had its place, but no more. It is rare that I even think about those thoughts that were ruling my life.

The reason we are miserable is that it is going against what is best for us, and we know that. We are at war with ourselves. Who is going to win? We have what is good for us at our taking or refusing.

Why do we struggle so? Why is the struggle even there? If we know what is best for us, why can't we just do what is best for us? That was the cross that Jesus faced for us. He conquered death, hell, and the grave. He was our example. He didn't say it would be easy to conquer our mind. He did say be yoked with Him, and His yoke is easy, and His burden is light. (Matt.11:30 KJV). We do not condemn ourselves. We are only thankful the truth was found to set us free.

5. People Are Seeking Peace

We can find peace, so we can go about our daily business with a free mind. We do not need to be afraid that God is pleased or displeased. We can be a free people to worship Him in spirit and truth. God is not a hard taskmaster. He would that we be in health and prosper, even as our soul prospers.

We can know that God has strength for us to do whatever task lies ahead. We have strength to do that task. We need only ask and seek to find the answer for surely the answer is there as we learn to accept what God has provided for us. Believing God's Word will calm our fears and give us confidence in our daily walk as we learn to listen to His voice.

6. God's Will

How will we know it is His will?
Can we do God's will?
What are the rewards of doing His will?

Recognizing His Will ... Is Our Will

How many times have I cried out, "What is God's will for my life?" I searched day and night for years. "God, let me know Your will."

This was one of my desperate times. I felt this time might be different. Maybe I could possibly get my answer once and for all. I did not plan on quitting until I found an answer. Many, many times before I received just enough knowledge for me to back off and feel satisfied for a season. But this time I was desperate. I needed to know God's will for my life. My health and well-being depended on an answer. I was gorging myself, overweight (that is a story in itself), so discontented and dissatisfied, not knowing where to go from here.

I did not know if it was God's will for me to write and share the truths I had written. I received help from the wisdom that I would write down, but then I shoved them back on a shelf, afraid to share. Truly, I was afraid to let others know of the raging storms inside me ... the real me. Why was I so weak in some ways and so very strong in others? I was afraid to share before I had all the answers.

For years I sought help for my weight problem. I believed there had to be an answer for all the overweight people. That night, as I lay down to sleep, the answer to losing weight seemed very insignificant; something more needful began to surface. This discontentment and unfulfilled feeling would be taken care of if I found God's will for my life. I wouldn't be dis-eased.

As I awoke the next morning, I began to think about Abraham, the father of many nations (Gal. 3:7 KJV). If Abraham is my father, then a loving and wise father lets his child decide what his or her vocation in life will be. The father teaches, disciplines, and gives wisdom to the child, whatever that task may be. The father steps back, and the child does the choosing. The child will have to carry out the work and see that it is accomplished. The child endures frustration, turmoil, and struggle before making the choice to follow and succeed.

I had my answer; it seemed so clear, so uncomplicated. How could I have been so blind to think God's will was some deep, dark mystery for my life? God had nurtured, led, and guided as I sought His face. Whatever I chose to do with what He freely gave me was my choice. He would stand behind, beside, and lead the way. God will uphold whatever I decide to do as I respond to the challenge.

I could not read the road signs along the way because of fear. But it was a comfort to know that God's will was my will all along, when my heart and mind were set on Him.

I had lots to give, but instead of giving, I kept hoarding great riches only to remain unsatisfied, unfulfilled, and miserable. Fear of inadequacy yet knowing deep inside what I learned would help someone else. I kept pondering, is *it really God's will that I write at this time?* I had so many avenues in my life in which it seemed my faith had not worked out for me. I wondered if others would look at those things and point a finger rather than receive the good I had to offer. Was experience really the best teacher? You see, I could always make up excuses. I used excuses to buffer me against the pressures, defeats, and setbacks. I was afraid what might happen if I opened myself to others.

Several years past I wrote this verse: "The secret of life you have found, keep giving forth so His love will abound." You would have thought I could have latched on to that truth and risen to heights unknown. Instead, I enjoyed the wisdom that I was receiving but kept it to myself, afraid, drawing back, hiding, secretly hoping to escape. But deep down, I wanted the courage to share.

God's Spirit is that measure of faith implanted within each of us to multiply and replenish the earth. We all can do God's will and succeed at something worthwhile, to have something to give to enrich the lives of others, whether it be spiritual or natural. We are spiritual beings in a natural body.

The greatest gift of all is giving of oneself. For in giving is contentment. Giving is the motivator in living a fulfilled life. There is not a way to stop the process of receiving when we give. It is a fact of life.

His will is not something that I have to fear. His will is my will, what I wanted to do all along but was too fearful. A door of confidence was immediately opened when I realized that my will was His will for my life.

What is so special about all of this is that God's will for my life is entirely different than His will for anyone else. I do not have to compare, be in competition, or disagree with someone else. We all have a place, and there does not have to be conflict. Room for all and all is needed to share what each one has learned. I have received encouragement from reading others' experiences. I believe we can learn from each other if we follow the dictates of our own hearts.

I realize it is not so important that I have all the answers. Each new experience brings unanswered questions. I can find contentment where I am today if I am willing to share. My fears, doubts, unbelief, misgivings all had to pass away and be buried, never to be remembered again. I was experiencing freedom, so I could live and give. God's Spirit and His words were always true. His yoke was easy and His burden light. It was fear that was so heavy to bear. God did not use might or power (guilt or condemnation). He gently led, even though it has taken years to show me the way. I can only say, "Thou art love, oh God! Thou art love!"

I need only to have a willing heart to see the need and seize the opportunity to share. I will never be a loser by giving.

7. Heaven Can Be Where You Make It

I do not wait until tomorrow to soar into the clouds.
I know my Savior lives within me this hour. I'm not waiting until after the sunset in life to look upon His face. My friend, He is here now.

If we really believe the scripture that reads, "Greater is He that is in us than he that is in the world" (1 John 4:4 KJV), we would live a life of victory instead of defeat. Fear would have to flee for the victory would have to prevail. We do not believe what we say.

He dwells within us, so we can overcome the evil that comes against us.

If He is peace, and if He dwells within us, then we shall know peace.
If He is love and He dwells within us, then we shall know love.
If He is patience and dwells within us, then we shall know patience.
If He is mercy and dwells within is, then we shall know mercy.

8. Good and Evil

We have within us the power to do good or evil.
Just as the cells in our blood rush toward the diseases that attack
our bodies, Gods word comes to our rescue to overcome the
evil that would destroy us.

Think upon things that are pure; good thoughts and feelings
will arise. Think upon things that are evil, and we will find
ourselves thinking about ways to let that evil come forth.

When we are overcome with evil, we find we would like not
to do evil, but it is hard to stop our thinking. We can cry out to
God, and by His grace and strength, we somehow pull through.
We may have gotten some scratches, but we are still alive,
and that is what counts. If there is life, there is hope. Christ
was an example of what can happen in our lives when we let
good overcome evil. Jesus had to pray that He enter not into
temptation. We can pray that we enter not into temptation.
Praying is the language of the soul. When we think on love,
our souls shed forth love. Our spirits are peaceful and loving.
Love causes our bodies to function like they should. It has been
proven that when we hate, our skin manufactures a poison. Hate
disrupts our beings. Hate and fear cause all kinds of sicknesses.
God gives us wisdom. The mind and spirit were meant to
communicate with God. Jesus was our example that this can
be done. God is in humankind. God can overcome evil, and we
can communicate with God.

Our actions are direct products of our minds. Either we can make the tree good or make it evil. We have a choice, and we have the power to do as we choose. We can overcome evil with good.

Faith and doubt cannot dwell together in peace.
We need only one Master. God's spirit within us can lead and guide us in whatever we need.

9. God's Children

Some of God's children are dissatisfied. Overweight, craving, but they know not what they are wanting. Eating but not feeling satisfied. Satisfaction only comes by giving of ourselves.

"Where do I start? What do I give?"

I don't have the answers for myself, so how can I give to someone else? As we get rid of fear, we can help each other. How many times have we answered the soul's cry by feeding the body? We end up not satisfying our soul but still stuffing our faces. If we are to be at peace with ourselves, we need to get to the root of the hunger.

The spirit of God within us is a giving spirit. We are not satisfied because we are not giving. We do not see our neighbor's needs; we see only our own distress. We hamper and cramp our growth by not seeing the needs of others. That hunger will never be stifled until we learn to give. He came not to do His will but His Father's. He comes within us to do the same. We are a spirit in this house of flesh and bones. This is only our earthy dwelling place.

We are a spirit; a spirit must be fed, nourished, and cared for. The spirit that is within us is a giving one and will not be satisfied any other way but by giving forth.

We cannot do anything to make us His children. We are His children. We are content when we are giving.

10. A Father Speaking to His Son

I made you in My image.
You are love, peace, joy.
You have fellowship with Me.
You are at My level.
You are accepted.
There isn't even a thought that you are not accepted.
I see you as perfect.
You are made in My image, and in Me there is no sin.
Your fleshly mind is against you being as I am.
That is why mercy endures forever.
The excellence of the Spirit is of Me.
You could ask what you will, but your mind will not let you.
Any fear you have is not of Me.
Let that same mind be in you that you think it not robbery to be a perfect Spirit in Mine eyes.
I see you as a perfect Spirit for you are in My image.
In God's eyes, you are not a failure, only in your eyes.
You are in this world, but you are not of this world.
Let love motivate you, not fear drive you.
Jesus knew who He was. He was a Son of God.

He was what His Father was.
You are a child of God; you are not a child of evil.
You have power over all power of the enemy when you realize who your Father is. Those who rebel against Me are children of their earthy father (fleshly mind). They follow their fleshly minds.

If you want to minister, do it because you love God's people, and the burden of your heart is to help them be free.

Do not minister because of fear. Fear that God will punish you if you do not speak. Do not let fear drive you to think you have to minister. Only minister if you have something to give that will help others to walk in love. When love burns within you so much that you want to help your fellow humans, then you will find a way to help them. That will be a duty of love, freely given and not driven by fear that you should be sharing. You will give because you want to give. You see the need, and you can fulfill that need. God never pushes or condemns. God leads the way with peace. If you feel rushed, it is not God. Remember, God knows what will be before it ever happens.

11. Faith and Trust

God helps us to choose faith and trust instead of doubt and fear. Both are set before us. We will be yoked with the stronger one, and the good within us will win out. We will be determined until that mind of distrust is brought into subjection.

His yoke is easy and His burden light. He brings life—not fear, doubt, and unbelief. He takes care of the lilies of the field. He sees the sparrow that falls. He hears us when we cry, and He speaks peace to our hearts, minds, and spirits.
He has been with us from the beginning.

We all have an inheritance. We can go into a far country and waste all that we have, even as the prodigal son. You notice he was still his son. He was his beloved son, even though he wasted all that He had given him, he was just as much of a son as the one who stayed and obeyed his father's wishes and rested in his father's wealth (Luke 15:20–32 KJV). He was not any less of a son because he ran away. The son paid a dear price for running and not believing his father. He did not believe that the best place to be was in his father's house.

The same reason Eve partook of the fruit in the garden, she did not believe her Father knew best (Gen. 3:6 KJV). Eve is the type of spirit taken out of man that pulls against the things that are best for us. It will pull, tear, rip, and destroy. We did not put ourselves in this place, so don't feel like a failure when you find yourself in bondage.

Our repentance is that we did not believe that God is in us. We do not follow His voice of trust but let fear lead us. The Spirit of God within us is to lead and guide, to make a way where there is no way. His Spirit does not hamper our lives, but shapes and molds us to glorify him and works only for our good.

Let Him be glorified in our lives. Let Him will and do of His own pleasure. God sent His Son to show us His inheritance. Jesus's inheritance did not fail Him. He was victorious over death, hell, and the grave.

We can believe that God's Spirit will arise and become Lord of our lives. He is victorious! He wrestled until His sweat became like droplets of blood, but He was victorious. Who will hold on when all odds are against us? Our spirit will hold as we are yoked with the greater power. We are on the winning side. We can fulfill our potential in life. Don't draw back.

We thank God for His mercy.
We thank God for His care.
We thank God for setting us free.
It is amazing how love lifts the heaviest load. High and be lifted with God, and He lifts us higher and higher.

When God's people find rest in their hearts and minds, they shall find peace in their bodies. God wills that we be in health and prosper even as our souls prosper.

If you understand that you have the mind of Christ, you can have peace that passes all understanding. When our hearts and minds are at peace, then our bodies are not dis-eased; we are at ease. Peace that surpasses all understanding is ours this day.

12. Loving Ourselves

How many times have we heard people say, "I am learning to love myself."

I have yet to find out what anyone has done to love himself or herself. Why hasn't someone shared how to do that?

It is one of the most important issues that anyone can have.

I haven't heard any answers. The only answer I have heard is, "No one else can make us love ourselves." If it was so easy, more people would be doing it. Why do we have to love ourselves? Why isn't someone else's love enough? If we love our families and give it all we have, why don't we feel satisfied? We do what we have been taught to do! What is the big deal? The big deal is taking up for and loving ourselves is, without a doubt, the number-one issue to our happiness.

The number one? Why? This goes back to the day we were born. We were born with that measure of faith. What is that measure of faith (Rom. 12:3 KJV)? That bit of faith makes us children of God. God is love, and He loves us with an everlasting love. A love that never wavers, never turns, and is an unconditional love. We need to return to our first love. "To become as a little child" (Matt. 18:3 KJV), with complete trust, complete trust for us to do what is best for us.

We can learn to love ourselves with a love that never lets us down. No matter how bad we want to do something, we will not allow ourselves to do anything if it is not for our good. We may have in the past given in to this desire. This time we will not do that. We will love ourselves too much to allow that to make us unhappy. We can declare our freedom by keeping our hearts and minds stayed upon our happiness.

We are kept in bondage by our thinking. Our minds can lay aside those things that so easily upset us for if we do not allow the thoughts, the actions will not follow. How do we do that? This must be by the Spirit, or it will not stand the test.

By the Spirit, by love, by loving ourselves enough to do what is ultimately the best for us.

Speaking God's words will put those unwanted thoughts to flight. "All things are possible if we believe" (Matt. 9:23 KJV). We can do all things through Christ, who strengthens us. We may have to speak those words several times until they become real to us. We know with surety His words will not return void. You will be surprised how quickly those thoughts will disappear.

13. Love Makes the World Go Around

Where are the real men of yesteryear?

The man who is honest, gentle, firm but kind, who disciplined a child when discipline was needed, but whose law was love; whose first love was God and family, one who was contented with the simple life.

The man who is willing to stand up and be counted when confronted with important decisions. Not for the name he made for himself, but because he is willing to give of himself to make this a better place to live.

The man who would rather have less and be able to go to bed and sleep at night, instead of staying awake worrying how the bills will be paid.

The man who would rather spend time with his family than to work overtime to give them material wealth to take his place.

Are the real men gone? Could there still be a trace of caring down deep in the heart of every man just waiting to spring forth?

Some men like for their wives to be as puppets: "Jump when I say jump!" A helpmate is not a puppet. If God meant for only men to have minds, He would not have given women one also. So many men are resentful and lash out at their wives. Most women try very hard to keep trouble down. They need each other, not to pull and tear at one another, but to help and understand daily problems.

When men come home from work, they want happy wives to greet them. Those weary and worn wives would like an encouraging word also. It is not one-sided if two are to live together in harmony. Who comforts the children when Dad comes home in a rage? A real man doesn't come home in a rage.

We have not taken time out for love. We will find time to fish, hunt, have extra jobs, bowl, golf, or work on an extra car, but we can't find time to fix a bike, repair a wagon, or put a bandage on a little girl's doll. If we take time to help someone when we are aggravated, it upsets everyone around us because we would rather be doing something else. Surely, the whole point of living is being bypassed.

Wives keep finding it harder to stand behind their husbands' decisions. Husbands work overtime to get that fine house or job, but they end up with ulcers or a coronary. Maybe the wife is under psychiatric counseling. What has really been gained? The result cannot be remedied with money. Money gets you there and then drops you off, leaving you stranded. You can't understand for the life of you how money has blinded. You started off with a good wife. You wanted to make her happy. You bought her material things, thinking that was what she wanted. We find out our hearts and minds were meant to thrive on love. When hate and resentment take over, communication breaks down.

If it could all be summed up, "rushing" would be the word best fitted to the occasion. Rushing is like a cancer, eating away at the home, blinding us, keeping us from taking time for the important values in life. Our ideals need to be reevaluated. What are we striving for? Will it pay in the end, or will we be left empty-handed when it comes to love?

It is as though there is one flag waving over our land today. It is a big dollar sign. Some of today's values are counterfeit. It is no wonder young people turn to drugs. They don't want to be in the same mess as their parents. They don't like hypocrisy but don't have the answers, so they jump from the frying pan into the fire.

It's not always the poor class of people whose children turn to drugs. In one school that I know, the first students to bring drugs into school were the three straight-A students. Making good grades is not enough; they need someone to care.

If a child is in sports, go watch that child participate. If the child is in music, go to the concerts. If he or she likes to hike, take a hike. If you are saying, "I have waited too long," you may be right. You will have to proceed with caution. At first, they will be very suspicious, but little by little, patience will win out. Have faith that love will win over that rebellious spirit. Don't add wood to the fire by telling a child you love him or her if you don't take time to listen to the child. If you buy a ball and bat, be prepared to play catch, even if it is only half hour at a time. How well they do is not as important as your being with them.

The man image we see today is not the image of God. God said, "Let us make man in our own image" (Gen. 1:26 KJV). The image we see is not a man of love and patience but one of hate and greed, rushing to get more earthly wealth. He doesn't realize his happiness lays right under his eyes, right in his own back door. It is often too late before he realizes that fact.

Where is the man who will ask forgiveness before closing his eyes at night instead of going to sleep, searing his conscience, that the chewing out he gave his family was coming to them? This left them miserable and tormented in their minds. There are cold, cruel, and heartless parents in this world with confused children starving for love.

We all have the capacity for love. Parents are so taken up with the crowd that they don't know what is proper and what is not. It is as if our ideals are turned upside down. We seem to be all part of the problem instead of part of the answer. We need a few parents who will step out of the rat race and dare to be as they feel they should be.

14. Searching for God

We need to search our Bibles to see if we are being told the truth. People will pay their last dollar to try to satisfy their spiritual needs. There were teachers here before Jesus came. Jesus didn't go along with all their forms, rites, and rituals. He just said, "Ask and ye shall receive" (Matt. 7:7 KJV). Be not afraid! Only believe (Mark 5:36 KJV). Jesus tells them they have left the weightier matters undone: "Love, mercy and judgment" (Matt. 23:23 KJV). You won't find what you are looking for in very many places today. You will find it in your heart when you read the Bible and pray.

Everybody's sins are forgiven. Jesus took care of that; the ultimate price has been paid. The only sins we need to repent of is not realizing Jesus lives within us. When breath was breathed into this body, we became a living soul. The fears and doubts and unbelief have kept us from believing. We were born with a measure of faith. There has been plenty of preaching done. Not enough truth and love shown that will cause people to be set free. Jesus paid the price! "Only believe, fear not only believe!" was Jesus's message when He spoke to the multitudes.

Jesus knew this fleshly mind was afraid to believe. Fear not! Fear not! Fear not! God sent His Son, Jesus, to show us what His Spirit in us is like. We are a son as Jesus is a Son. We can have love for our fellow humans as Jesus had love when we realize we are pleasing God. God is working for our ultimate good. God tried to show Moses's people that He could walk and talk with them. He tried to show Adam and Eve, but they couldn't believe. He gave the ultimate sacrifice of His Son to show us that we are His children.

God does not need our money. He does need us to be a vessel of love.

I remember a story about a woman who did not go to church regularly. The church people kept nagging at her and telling her she should be in church to live a Christian life. But she continued to miss services. Finally, some of the church people decided to check up on her to see where she was. They found her busy, helping a needy family. Her religion was not in attending church but in living love.

We can gather together in church to encourage and build our faith. Salvation is a way of life, not a form or doctrine. Many people are deceived by thinking church attendance and leadership are the answers. It is good, but they are not the answers. Receiving God's gift of love is the only answer. The message is so plain and simple it is overlooked.

When Jesus was born of Mary and Joseph, not many knew of His birth. The same way it is today. When love is born in you, it is a silent thing as far as the world is concerned. To you, it is life and peace. It is as a live coal of fire, lighting hearts wherever it goes. We only need to tell of His love, coming to earth to redeem us. God's Spirit is in everyone; they just haven't realized that fact. Our deeds tell more than our talk will ever say.

Doctrines come and go and change, but the Bible and God remain the same. When people find God for themselves, they know they have met the Master. You don't have to preach condemnation when they have met the Master. His love is so great, we don't even think about not obeying Him.

People go to church because they are searching. Maybe they don't even know what they are searching for. Our souls cry out for their Maker. But churches are afraid to teach something different from what they were taught. Paul had to go away to listen to God.

If we aren't very careful, we will be building monuments in our names, thinking we are doing God's work. If we stop and really look at what is happening, it has nothing to do with God's kingdom.

Remember the prayer He taught His disciples: "For thine is the Kingdom, and the power and the glory forever" (Matt. 6:13 KJV). It is God's kingdom in each one of us. It is God's power that dwells within, and God will not share His glory.

Who are we to obey? Who is our Father? Who is our Master? Who wants to be our Teacher and wants us to ask and seek until we find? It would be great to hear we can go straight to the teacher and find a fountain that flows deep and wide. God and His love for us do not change. When God's love is bought with money, it only fails and passes away. If the gospel of peace was taught, the churches would not hold the people. They are that hungry.

Don't be afraid to seek God. Renew your mind. Our minds do not know the things of God. Our minds are against God's mind. That is why we need to get rooted and grounded in His Word, not in what someone has taught us. Oh, it seems right, but it may not be God's way.

Church is a wonderful place to teach people about the Spirit of God that dwells within each of us. To teach people to get God's Word rooted and grounded in their hearts and minds. There is no respect of persons. We don't hear that very often. Everyone has that measure of faith that was breathed into them. They need to share the truth of how to water that bit of faith and show how it will grow and supply all their needs. How to get rooted and grounded in His Word. The Word never fails us. He is our Comforter. As we seek and as we find, we can share what God has taught us and be a blessing to encourage others to search the Word for themselves.

There is room for all. Open your mind to the Master to listen and learn. It is a proven fact that "If you seek you will find. If you knock it shall be opened unto you. If you ask you shall receive" (Luke 11:9 KJV). It is our Father's great pleasure to give us His kingdom. We are His temple; He dwells within. It is free to all.

God's words are life. They are living words. They can erase fear. His words can calm our raging thoughts. His words can cause peace to sweep over our souls. His words can cause our enemies to flee. His words lift. His words propel us forward and upward at the same time.

King David hid God's Word in his heart so he would not sin against God (Psalm 119:11 KJV). What sin was David talking about? He was not listening to his heavenly Father. Also, David had to encourage himself when he was discouraged. How did David encourage himself? He spoke the Word hidden within his heart. He could have called in all the counselors in his kingdom, but he had the Counselor living within himself.

The Word that we hide within our hearts comes to our rescue in a flash. God promised to bring it to our remembrance. We not only remember it, it works. He says His Word would not return void. His Word is so full of life that once you start studying it, one scripture leads to another, and the first thing you know, a whole new world has opened just for you. His Word is life itself. What His Word teaches you may be different than what others have taught you. Just keep believing what His Word shows and tells you, and it will bring life. There will never be any condemnation, only peace.

We can only believe what our faith allows us to believe. Maybe your faith is different from others' faith. We are all raised by different parents and many beliefs. God gets to each of us where we are in life. We do not have to compare ourselves to anyone. When people ask us, we can share what we have learned. Some will jump for joy; others just can't grasp what we learned. That is okay. God's Spirit is in them the same as in us.

As we seek His face, He will lead and guide us to all truth. We are all at different places in our lives, and only God knows what our needs are. There is no room for guilt or condemnation, only understanding and peace. If God doesn't open our eyes so we can see, we are not going to see. It is all by His Spirit.

15. God's Wisdom

God wills that His people be in health and prosper. He wishes for them the best. He desires for them to know Him in His fullness. He is mercy, peace, forbearing, long-suffering, gentleness, and kindness.

His words are that mercy shall follow us all the days of our life, and we shall dwell in His house (Psalm 23:6 KJV).

God has miracles awaiting the minds of His people. He wills that we not perish in our minds. God equips His people with what is necessary to meet their needs.

There is not a door we cannot open if we are willing to open our minds. God's wisdom is unlimited to those that trust their minds to Him. He will never lead us in the wrong direction. Many times, we need to wait for His guidance. He says if we wait upon Him, He shall renew our strength.

16. Know Yourself

Some people can be so cruel and heartless. They are unstable and will do all they can to rock your boat. Misery truly loves company. Love and trust do not thrive around fear, doubt, and unbelief. They are leeches, sapping our lives. There is only one way to truly be happy. We will go all around, go under it, trample over it, and do everything but trust. True happiness stems from within. We must conquer the fear of what people think. Are we truly happy with ourselves? Are we doing the best we can without envy and strife? Is love our motivation? If love is the answer, then we must be truly blind to other opinions. For other opinions may pull you down. If one out of ten encourages you, you have beaten the odds. With that kind of percentage, you may find doubts mounting within you that will drag you back farther than you gained.

If you are entirely true with yourself and have found your place in life, don't take what people think of you too seriously. You and you alone know you. You will find that the one who criticizes the most never has the facts. Facts will always change the picture. Giving advice when it isn't asked for usually causes more contention and strife. If someone asks for advice, the person is ready to receive. Spreading your knowledge around doesn't help anyone but your ego. Of course, you can always say, "I told you so," if that helps. There are other ways of helping people without giving advice. Listening to someone's problems can cause a new outlook and change the whole perspective of the problem.

17. Fear Is Being Taught in Many Religions

Hades: A place of fire and brimstone, with the devil and his angels tormenting his victim day and night throughout all eternity. We have heard this preached in many churches. The fact remains we do not have to wait until we die to suffer in torment. God does not use fear to draw us to Him.

When fear grips us, we are tormented day and night; it burns away at our lives. Just because we have been taught a certain doctrine does not make it truth. It seems like we are gluttons for punishment the way we allow our minds to dwell on fear. We are in a living torment when we create images in our minds that are not peaceful. If what we believe hampers and confuses, torments and hinders our well-being, we need to rid ourselves from the jaws of torment.

A life shadowed and driven by fear is not an abundant life. We were intended to know love, power, and a sound mind. Fear is the last enemy to be put down for fear causes death. Fear causes death to love, death to trust, and death to life thinking. We were not born with the spirit of fear. We were born with the spirit of trust. The kind of fear that comes by loving is reverence and respect, not a tormenting fear.

The simplicity of love is overlooked and made complicated. Love is the expression of one's self. Free to be you. When you find you, you will find that you are a product of love. We all come into this life the same way—a wriggly, pink form, struggling to find comfort. Since we are bundles of love, only love will make us grow and mature like we are meant to do. Without love, we become distorted and deformed in our thinking.

As of now, few are being reared on pure love. We end up with many hang-ups to further complicate our lives. When we find ourselves, we will come face-to-face with God. If we know God when we leave this earth, we won't have to worry about literal torment.

Wars and Rumors of Wars, Earthquakes, and Famines

We will have wars and rumors of wars, thoughts and torments coming against our peace. There are times when we are shaken for a season. We shall stand as we sort out our fears from truth. Abraham was continually pulling up stakes as he covered new ground. He wasn't satisfied to stay in one place. Ever learning and finding new truth is putting together the puzzle of our lives. Doctrines we have been taught will be shaken, and what is truth will remain strong. We will have wars and rumors of wars, earthquakes, and famines. These are facts of life. We have these spiritually and naturally.

Fear of Death

The fear of death gets its sting from what we have been taught about after-death experiences. Since we realize where torment can be, the fear of death lost its grip. You can be dead and in the grave while still walking upon this earth. We can be so bogged down by fears that you do not feel alive. Our fears have us in our graves, not able to live and let live. Learning the truth, we can break out of those graves and shake off the grave clothes from our minds and begin living again. We need to understand unbelief for what it is, a robber of our joy and peace. We give ourselves unnecessary punishment by condemnation. The way we think influences our whole course of life. We can let fear disappear and receive peace as our reward. God is love and mercy. God never leaves us; it's our minds that separate us from God. Be good to yourself. Be true to yourself. We will not truly enjoy being good to others until we have learned to be good to ourselves. Don't be tormented in your mind. Learn to let your being dwell in peace.

Fear in Prayer and Fasting

We will find our spirit needs food as our bodies need food. We will find ourselves very agitated and unfulfilled if our souls are not getting fed. We will not be able to combat our fears and guilt if we have not given our spirits the Word from God that they need. To help free someone else we need to learn what it is to free our own minds and spirits. Our insides cry out to be free from bondage. The essence of our prayer is to loosen the bindings that teachings have placed upon us.

Fear of How to Dress

We can wear our dresses down to the floor and still be afraid within. Our hair can be long, and maybe never cut, and we still may not have peace of mind. Long dresses and long hair can be drudgery for some and an unnecessary burden we can lay down. We really do not need to spend so much time considering what we put on or take off. If we are not clothed with peace, courage, and fortitude, what we wear doesn't make for happiness.

Fear of Baptism

The baptism that is needful is to be immersed with trust. To be covered so fear does not creep in. It will bombard us at times. John the Baptist's message was one of a new knowledge: Repent, the kingdom of God is at hand (Matt. 3:2 KJV). Repent from what? Repent from not believing God is in us. Jesus was sent for the sole purpose of showing we are children of God, even as He was. The kingdom of God is not of this earth; it is within humankind. Humanity's rules and regulations have nothing to do with this kingdom.

Fear Is Gone

Fear will flee for it is not grounded in truth. When truth comes, fear takes leave. If love motivates us to do something and we are afraid, then fear is still the conqueror. Begin by speaking the truth to yourself, tell yourself why you want to do this one thing, and why it is so important to you. Push through, and you will see that your fears were ungrounded. The one rule to start getting rid of fear is to ask yourself if your intentions are good. If your intentions are good, fear has no hold. We begin to see that fear is only as big as we let it appear to us.

Now that fear is taken out of worshipping God, what have we left? If we don't have rules and regulations, will we go off the deep end? Many questions will haunt you. Answer those questions with the new hope you have acquired. God does not give us the spirit of fear, but of power and love and a sound mind. His words will always lift our spirits with peace. Love will not fail us. Love is our God-given nature.

Fear of the Second Coming of Jesus

Faith (spirit) is within us when we are born and gets covered over; we crucify it many times. When we finally let faith overcome unbelief, then our spirits arise from the dead, and He has come again to us. He comes to sit on His throne within us. He comes in great glory if we let him. Only comfort and peace He brings. That is too simple for some to accept. When He comes, He opens the graves in our hearts and minds and gives us new life.

When we believe, we do not need to fear His literal coming.

18. The Birthplace of Violence

If you were one of the few whose parents never raised their voices to discipline you, you are one of the very fortunate. They probably corrected you by telling you what you were doing wrong. No violence or force was used, only fairness by the parents by being an example and winning respect. I made a lot of mistakes while raising my two children. Even if we do the best we know how to do, it doesn't mean we always do the right thing.

If parents fight, yell, scream, pull, jerk, and slap to get what they want, their children will do the same. We have precious lives in our care. If we push and shove by example, what do we expect from our children?

We could be better parents by not embedding the fears we have into our children. Children see our fears and do not understand. Soon they are fashioning their lives the same way. It is a shame that we care more about what others think than we do about what our family thinks about us. There does not seem to be a consistency to our lives. We say one thing and do another.
Some of the most simple and beautiful answers to important questions come from children. If you are having a problem, ask their opinion. Nine times out of ten, you will get a good answer. Children are quick to take an active part in family problems if given a chance.

When our child goes wrong, we tend to blame the crowd he or she runs with. Your child is also a part of that crowd that someone else's child runs with. The home determines whether your child will be violent.

We went through the permissive stage, where we were told not to discipline our children. We listened to doctors tell us that. Now we blame the psychiatrists. The underlying truth is they told us exactly what we wanted to hear. It is easier at the time to let children do as they please. The rewards for those actions were very heartbreaking. Children began to believe their parents did not love them or they would set boundaries. They had no charted course to follow, only a blind alley. Left alone to do their thing was very boring when no one cared. Then the gap of communication began to widen. Most of all, children need someone to listen and to guide them by example. Then we can hear them voice their underlying fears.

We can be brought up above our fears and doubts. We can sit in heavenly places (peace and joy, no sorrow added). The account of Jesus's life is a record of showing us God's Spirit dwells within us today. He gave His life and showed us He conquered all that we are faced with. We stop our way of thinking, so we can have an abundant life.

19. Words of Strength

Confrontation—Confront our problems every day squarely in the face. Meet them on the grounds of what we can and are willing to do.

Convalescing—We are recuperating from the rites and rituals we have heard all our lives. We need to rise, shine and dictate our own lives. We need to take control and know the power we possess. We can push through the mountains of difficulties and arrive victoriously on the opposite side.

We can make a way where before there seemed to be no way. We may have to start from scratch, but scratch is better than nothing; even though it may appear as nothing, it is something. We may have to gather together, pluck from here and there, but a few fragments do remain.

Discipline—Discipline is self-control or to teach oneself obedience. Obedience is submission to a command or law. It may even be contrary to what we believe, sometimes held by fear.

Give our children the well-used tools of digging out, shaping up, and tunneling through the obstacles that come against us each day. Show them that you are not escaping reality but are facing life head-on with courage and fortitude. Show them how to attain happiness and peace. We all face the same difficulties and joys in life. Some are just more courageous in attending to their responsibilities. When we take responsibility for our actions, we find we have more mercy on others around us.

We go to great extremes to keep from facing responsibility. As we rule, our destinies are we going to be content to pass on the heritage to our children we now find in ourselves. Or will we start coping with our problems by facing them and digging our way through the mountains. Or we will continue to escape, leaving our children without any tools or knowledge to have courage to face reality and not run. Our children need to know the steps to meet crises that arise. They only know by watching us as we meet our challenges.

Are we successful, resourceful, determined, or are we quitters? Do we run from our problems and blame someone else for them?

Do we face our responsibilities, admitting our faults and finding a way? Or do we turn back before we are winners?

Learning to be strong in the little problems gives us strength not to collapse when confronted with crises.

Truth—Truth is real. Truth for God's people to believe in, for truth is a workable system destined to survive.

Character—That is what we need. There is protection in standing up for what we believe. We can latch on to it. When we stand up for what we believe, others will take courage and reevaluate their lives. There is strength in multitudes.

Reinforcement—Strict reinforcement is our strength. Not wavering, being tossed around. With reinforcement, strength is multiplied and increased. Reinforcement here a little and there a little, and strength is ours in magnitude.

Principles—Rules and policies are very important to our growth. We can chart our courses. We can have guidelines set to lead and guide us. Adhere to the moral standards we set for ourselves, not to what someone else sets up for us or what they go by. Moral standards are ours to uphold.

Combination of strength and durability—Not neglecting the values that make for real happiness and contentment in our lives. Learning to protect ourselves from setbacks and pitfalls that cramp and bind us in many ways. Not neglecting to destroy the monsters we have created in our fearful way of life that draw our strength and sap our walk of faith.

Preparation—We derive strength within the guidelines that we set. We prepare for the battles that lie ahead. "We can know in whom we have believed." (2Tim. 1:12 KJV) God is able to take care of us in all things.

Some beliefs can draw us away from facing reality and having the right perspective. We deal with real problems each day. We can have discernment and knowledge of how to deal with those experiences and crises.

Fortitude—Strength of mind that enables a person to encounter danger or bear pain or adversity with courage.

We need that inner discipline of our minds and emotions and not let them ramble off into if or what-ifs but make straight paths for our feet.

Insight – Discernment and the ability to see into the depths of a situation. We need insight into our problems, not by some magical force, but by taking them apart piece by piece.

Not knowing the circumstances cause fear. When we take apart an obstacle, we gain knowledge about it, and fear is dispelled.

Successful—We can be overcome, or we can succeed. When we press through, we find there is truth in the words (nothing is impossible to those who believe). We only let it be impossible by not tackling the situation. All things are possible. We can face life straightforward by not imagining failures but by planning for winning and success.

We achieve success; it doesn't just happen. When we arrive and succeed, we know how we got there.

Superfluous—Exceeding what is necessary or extravagant.

Don't be extravagant in our needs and wants. We know that is not what makes for happiness. Knowledge of the truth is what brings happiness.

Superfluous wants and needs affect only the surface. "On the surface," presents only an appearance without substance or significance. Keeping up an outward appearance by not seeing into or not having a sense of belonging can make one miserable inside and very shallow. When we are shallow, we do not delve into the truths about our fears and shortcomings.

We are afraid of what we will find. The fear of what we will find is the doorkeeper, causing us to be kept from the truth.

We are our own worst enemy. We have the power within us to free ourselves, but we don't dare trust our feelings and be led out of our prison walls. We have the key—courage—but we don't dare insert it into the lock because it might fail. What have we got to lose? We are in prison now. If it fails, we will stay in prison. But it will not fail; it is destined to succeed. It is tried and proven to be true. No gimmicks; it is an open-and-shut case. It will work. We can free ourselves from fears and doubts that were instilled in us along the way.

Make your way through the crowd. Weave in and out, cut a hole in the roof and go down in, crawl under, and tunnel through. But don't stop until you find a way. There is room on the other side, and you will know freedom.

Security—Comes from facing reality. Reality is seeing things as they really are. Know where the enemy is. Don't exaggerate or imagine what might have been or could be.

To survive we are going to have to know how to do it, what tools to use. We must assess the situation and take inventory of what we have. We need to start using what we possess and then add to and enlarge our boundaries.

Heritage—We do not want to leave our children and grandchildren a heritage of fear, doubt, and unbelief.
When our beliefs are shackled by fear, hampered by doubts (delusions and illusions), and evade the truth, we may find ourselves trusting in objects, believing something complicated and unknown. We may ignore simplicity.
How we ever got ourselves into this predicament is hard to realize. Traditions and customs can be filled with untruths and

falsehoods. We have not because we ask not. We can question, test, and see the results. Trial and error. Nothing ventured, nothing gained.

We must keep our heads and feet planted solidly and have control of our thinking. Do not let fear bind your thinking. Believe yourself, your spirit, and your God. Do not entertain fears and traditions unless they work for you. Do not add to your misery by running from reality. The heritage we leave our children depends entirely on what our beliefs and character display.

Sacrifice—Often the answer to having what you desire. To sacrifice is to surrender something for the sake of something else. We must sacrifice what we desire to take care of first things first to keep our lives in order.

Resistance—Is our friend.

With God's Word hidden within our hearts, we have the knowledge to resist whatever is not working for our good. God wants us to be in health and to prosper. Knowing this, we can have confidence. As we speak His Word, we come against all thoughts that would discourage our progress. When we have done what we know to do, we stand for what is right.

Reality—Rises above fantasy.

We can have a vision.

We can daydream, but with reality as our foundation.

We can build on dreams and have goals and visions to better humankind.

We can be the one to pull the strings that make our dreams happen.

Fantasy—Free play of our minds; floating around in space; shutting out problems, pain, and suffering. Not wanting to believe that pain and suffering are as much a part of real life as happiness.

Discomfort should be tackled with the same vigor and enthusiasm. As we realize our integrity, we become stronger for having overcome obstacles. Happiness comes in various forms and disguises. There is still only one that completely satisfies. In putting all you have into the accomplishment, you will know you gave it your best.

Judgment—Rarely helps and usually leaves condemnation if it is not accompanied by a solution.
I see many blaming others, finding fault. What are the solutions to the faults they found? Do they have the healing salve to rub on the wound and stop the bleeding? Or are they just able to see the wound and feel helpless to do anything about it?

You may say one can't change anything. No one is alone when one tells one and two tells two and three tells three and four tells four. If we remain faithful at our posts, changes begin to happen. If we are going to set ourselves up as judges, let us pass judgments that will be instrumental in making this a better place to live.

Let us start where the battle is the greatest—in our own minds. When we have fought a good fight on the front line or firing line, we will be capable of healing our brothers and sisters.

Faith without works is dead. Believing God *can do* something is not enough. Believing God *will do* something is putting works with our faith.

The GOSPEL OF PEACE is like the FRUIT THAT IS RIPE IS ALWAYS SWEETER.

Printed in the United States
By Bookmasters